CREATING INTERIOR ATMOSPHERE

CREATING INTERIOR ATMOSPHERE

MISE-EN-SCÈNE AND INTERIOR DESIGN

JEAN WHITEHEAD

BLOOMSBURY VISUAL ARTS
LONDON • NEW YORK • OXFORD • NEW DELHI • SYDNEY

BLOOMSBURY VISUAL ARTS
Bloomsbury Publishing Plc
50 Bedford Square, London, WC1B 3DP, UK
1385 Broadway, New York, NY 10018, USA
29 Earlsfort Terrace, Dublin 2, Ireland

BLOOMSBURY, BLOOMSBURY VISUAL ARTS and the Diana logo
are trademarks of Bloomsbury Publishing Plc

First published in Great Britain by Bloomsbury Visual Arts 2018
Reprinted 2021, 2024

Cover design: Louise Dugdale
Cover image: Getty Images/John Kobal Foundation

A catalogue record for this book is available from the British Library.

Library of Congress Cataloging-in-Publication Data
Names: Whitehead, Jean, author.
Title: Creating interior atmosphere: mise en scène and interior design /
Jean Whitehead.
Description: New York: Bloomsbury Visual Arts, 2018.
Identifiers: LCCN 2016036831 | ISBN 9781474249676 (pbk.: alk.paper)
Subjects: LCSH: Interior decoration–Psychological aspects.
Classification: LCC NK2113 .W49 2017 | DDC 747.001/9–dc23
LC record available at https://lccn.loc.gov/2016036831

ISBN: PB: 978-1-4742-4967-6
ePDF: 978-1-4742-4968-3
eBook: 978-1-4742-4969-0

Typeset by Saxon Graphics Ltd, Derby
Printed and bound in Great Britain

To find out more about our authors and books visit
www.bloomsbury.com and sign up for our newsletters.

With special thanks to:
Alan, without whose unstinting support and ability to undertake
all domestic duties this book would never have happened, and
my colleague David Losasso, who finally called my bluff on that
book I always said I was going to write … this is the result!

Contents

Chapter One

Creating interior atmosphere
An introduction

9 Introduction
10 What is interior design?
13 Scope of this book
– interior design and
mise-en-scène
15 What is atmosphere?
18 Conclusion
19 Further reading
– exploring atmosphere

Chapter Two

What's in a room?
The principles of
mise-en-scène

21 The power of the interior
21 What is mise-en-scène?
26 What is an interior
mise-en-scène?
38 Conclusion
39 Further reading
– exploring
mise-en-scène

Chapter Three

The interior setting
The backdrop or
'skin' of the space

41 What is an interior
setting?
41 What is the physical
environment – the skin?
47 Examples of interior
mise-en-scène, creating
an interior setting
48 Case Study One: The
Cabinet of Dr. Caligari
50 Case Study Two: Rough
Luxe Hotel
53 Case Study Three:
Strawberry Hill
56 Case Study Four:
'Re-Set'
59 Case Study Five: KU64
Kids Club
62 Conclusion
63 Further reading
– exploring the interior
setting

Chapter Four

What is an interior 'prop'?
Accessories,
furniture, fixtures
and equipment

65 Introducing interior
props
65 Using interior props
71 Examples of interior
mise-en-scène, props
and atmosphere
72 Case Study One: The
Ace Hotel
74 Case Study Two: *A
Clockwork Orange*
76 Case Study Three: Break
Down
79 Case Study Four:
Maggie's Cancer Caring
Centre
81 Case Study Five:
Kesselskramer
84 Conclusion
85 Further reading
– exploring interior
props

Chapter Five

Special effects
Interior space and experiences

Chapter Six

Light and shadow
Uncovering its dramatic role

Chapter Seven

Colour
A Technicolor© inner world

87 Introducing interior special effects
87 Special effects – perception and atmosphere
93 Examples of interior mise-en-scène and their special effects
94 Case Study One: *Dogville*
96 Case Study Two: La Maison Champs Elysées
100 Case Study Three: Fragrance Lab for Selfridges
103 Case Study Four: *Citizen Kane*
105 Case Study Five: Alcoholic Architecture
108 Conclusion
109 Further reading – considering special effects

111 Introducing light and shadow
111 Lighting and atmosphere
117 Examples of interior mise-en-scène – using light and shadow
118 Case Study One: *Nosferatu*
120 Case Study Two: 'The Weather Project'
123 Case Study Three: D.E. Shaw and Co. Offices
126 Case Study Four: Sam Wanamaker Playhouse
128 Case Study Five: The West Lobby in The Cosmopolitan
130 Conclusion
131 Further reading – exploring light and shadow

133 Introducing colour
133 Colour and atmosphere
141 Examples of interior mise-en-scène, using colour
142 Case Study One: *The Cook, The Thief, His Wife and Her Lover*
144 Case Study Two: Spiegel Publishing Headquarters
146 Case Study Three: 'Dots Obsession'
148 Case Study Four: The Hotel
150 Case Study Five: Wards 23 and 29, Bradford Royal Infirmary
152 Conclusion
154 Further reading – exploring colour

155 Endnotes
161 Bibliography
167 Index
172 Picture credits
174 Acknowledgements

1 Creating interior atmosphere

An introduction

We perceive atmosphere through our emotional sensibility – a form of perception that works incredibly quickly, and which we humans evidently need to help us survive … We are capable of immediate appreciation, of a spontaneous emotional response, of rejecting things in a flash.[1]

(Zumthor, [2006] 2015: 13)

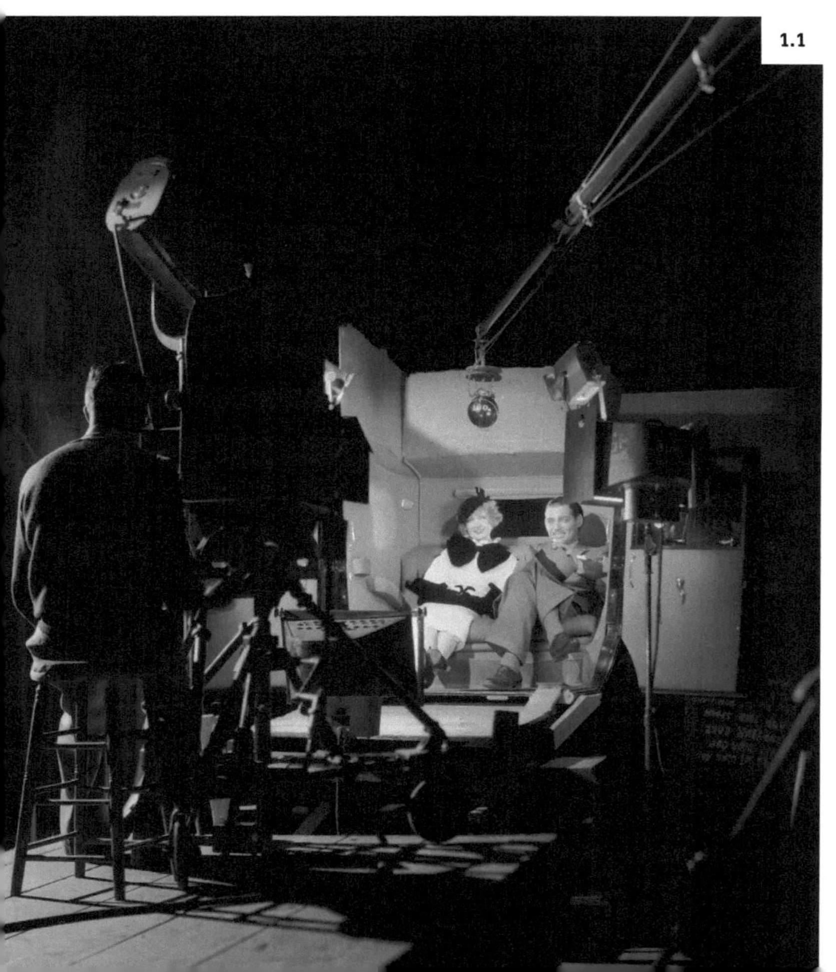

1.1

Figure 1.1
Burke and Gable – Clark Gable and Billie Burke act out a scene in the back seat of a limousine for the romantic comedy *Forsaking All Others*, directed by W. S. Van Dyke.
By considering the theatrical origins and cinematic context of mise-en-scène the notion of 'staged space' can theoretically be applied to the consideration and design of interior atmosphere.

Introduction

What is this book about? In essence, this book aims to revisit interior decoration, an often marginalized aspect of interior design, by exploring the notion of the decorated interior as one of staged space. In fact, it would be even more accurate to say that this book examines and is naturally drawn to theatrical examples of staging within a cinematic context, largely because of the affinity of the stage set and production design with the study of interiors. But this is about more than just the 'physicality' of the stage set. By gazing at interior space through the lens of 'mise-en-scène' (pronounced *meez-ahn-sen*), this book aims to show how this can simultaneously increase your understanding of the interior setting, whilst contributing to the creation of an intense interior atmosphere. Workable definitions of mise-en-scène are many and varied, and they will be discussed in more detail in later chapters, but the simplest definition owes much to an audience's perception of a given scene, so:

mise-en-scène is indeed the art of framing, choreographing and displaying – and an essential part of this, in many films of many different kinds, happens in what is staged (predominantly, actors in an environment) for a camera.[2]

(Martin, 2014: 15)

This suggests that an interior setting in the cinema is designed to be expressive; you could argue that this has become its second nature. It aims to set the scene, deepening our understanding of the characters, whilst the use of narrative or storytelling forms an integral component of this type of environment. Production designers working alongside directors create illusory filmic settings in which we as the audience can emotionally invest. Carefully constructed man-made sets or adapted locations undoubtedly help to set the tone of a film by spatially reinforcing its narrative or characterization. This approach to the interior could easily be referred to as one of 'staged space'.

Interiors can also be coaxed to tell a story and this becomes yet another point of reference to mise-en-scène. Narrative is increasingly used by interior designers; within the commercial sector it is harnessed to convey the essence of a brand. Retail 'brand-scapes' are deliberately aspirational, often memorable, aiming to communicate the brand ethos through a carefully considered arrangement of graphics, lighting and setting that aims to appeal to the core customer. The work of 'experience' designers Bompas and Parr and of exhibition designers Traast + Gruson falls readily into this category.

Interiors also have the power to surprise and delight, welcome, intimidate or even subdue. As designers we can create spaces that are more than the sum of their built parts. We can put together an interior 'setting' that aims to evoke a certain feeling or emotion through its harnessing of interior atmosphere. This is just another type of narrative albeit a psychological one, a form of interior storytelling as expressed by a certain ambience or notion of habitation. Maggie's Cancer Caring Centres in Britain offer support to anyone with, or affected by, cancer. They have successfully assimilated the archetypal qualities of the domestic home into the design of their interiors, in the creation of a psychologically familiar and inviting space. The work of the architect Daniel Libeskind, especially the interiors of his Jewish Museum in Berlin, or his evocative reworking of the heart of Ground Zero in New York, resonates with this approach.

So, is it all questions of semantics – does space communicate? It certainly does not speak in the literal sense, but it can murmur softly in our ear, whispering suggestions, conjuring a mood, evoking emotions and responses. This book will explore a way of thinking about, analysing, and creating interior space for the interior designer that owes a debt to the world of film. This will begin through an analysis and evaluation of mise-en-scène's relevance to the interior. It aims to place interior decoration as the lost prodigal son squarely back into any discussion regarding interior design.

What is interior design?

An interior designer is a creative problem solver who can think three-dimensionally and has mastered the atmospheric potential of interior space.

The prevailing focus for this chapter is highlighted next, which will begin through a response to the question 'what is interior design?'.

CHAPTER FOCUS

- An examination of the specialism of interior design and the role of the interior designer.
- An introduction to the concept of 'staged space' within interior design.
- An exploration of the term 'atmosphere' within the context and study of interior design.

Questions often asked by students and other interested parties are 'what does an interior designer do?' and 'what is the scope of their work?'. The answers are surprisingly complex, and rather contentious, as there is a general air of confusion over the terms 'interior designer', 'interior decorator' and 'interior architect'. In reality, the difference between these three terms is not finite as it alters in response to the country any designer is operating from. For example, some countries regulate their interior design profession whilst others do not. The British Institute of Interior Design (BIID) recently adopted the International Federation of Interior Architects/Designers (IFI) description in an attempt to define the role of the interior designer. This becomes a useful starting point and their definition is as follows:

Identify, research and creatively solve problems pertaining to the function and quality of the interior environment. Perform services relating to interior spaces including programming, design analysis, space planning, aesthetics and inspection of work on site, using specialized knowledge of interior construction, building systems and components, building regulations, equipment, materials and furnishings. Prepare schematics, drawings and documents relating to the design of interior space, in order to enhance the quality of life and protect the health, safety, welfare and environment of the public.[3]

(IFI World, n.d.)

This description serves as an introduction to the professional world of the interior designer and provides a sharp contrast to the role of the interior decorator as a clear distinction can now be made. Whilst the decorator typically concentrates solely on the look and feel of an interior environment, they are less concerned with developing a cohesive site and user response as this is seen as the preserve of the designer.

Within the profession certain specialisms exist, defined by an interior designer's personal preferences, or perhaps dictated by the type of work the design consultancy that employs them are known for. The two main sectors remain 'residential' (concentrating on all permutations of the domestic sphere) versus 'commercial' (typically retail, exhibition design, hospitality and entertainment, healthcare or educational, as well as workplace design). In the quest to create useful working definitions that relate to the interior decorator, the interior architect and the interior designer, it will be relevant to explain each title or role separately. Because of the protected status relating to the title of 'architect', the term interior architect does not exist professionally within Britain (although once again this varies depending upon where you are geographically). The three suggested categories are deliberately broad in their definition and are written with the proviso that there are always exceptions to any given rule; they simply offer a differing career specialism for any budding interior designer.

Interior decoration and the interior decorator

Like it or loathe it, this is most people's first impression of interior design because it dominates the television schedules and glossy, coffee-table magazines. Almost everyone has a home they enjoy tinkering with and updating in line with current trends, so does that make everyone an interior decorator? Interior decoration has certainly become synonymous with the home through the refurbishment of residential design schemes. It can, however, easily spill over into other design sectors, especially if the budget is limited and only a purely decorative approach can be undertaken or is required to refresh the space. It concentrates on the application of surface finish and colour, the acquisition of furniture, lighting and accessories to create a specific look. The chosen decoration can be closely aligned with the personal style of a specific designer or the prevailing taste of a client, whilst it is not uncommon for a realized scheme to closely follow particular fads or fashions. There is also a strong link to home-styling shops with the interior decorator often operating from a base that is part design studio, part office and part retail environment.

Decorators tend to work closely with their clients, taking a brief and developing mood boards and drawings to communicate their ideas; they are adept 'shoppers', understanding how to 'assemble' an interior through carefully selected props and accessories. The refitting of a kitchen, bathroom or other built-in fixtures (often bespoke), whilst working alongside a builder, is not uncommon in this sector. The predominance of 'softer' materials such as textiles, the use of paint and wall coverings, through to the selection of furniture and lighting are all central to this approach. Interior decoration has a strong association with the theatrical 'staging' of space in the creation of interior atmospheres through memorable 'scenes' or rooms.

Interior architecture and the interior architect

Interior architecture, in contrast, approaches the design of the interior through its relationship to, and interdependence with, architecture. It aims to promote a holistic design solution that is embedded in its understanding of a specific site (or building). Interior architecture sought to differentiate itself from the role of the decorator at a time when interior decoration and interior design had become increasingly confused professionally. By carefully considering the original building, interior architecture aims to develop an appropriate architectural response rather than one of 'superficial' applied ornamentation – an accusation often levelled at the interior decorator. Clearly, this approach has a close association with certain architectural theories, principles and tactics, and this knowledge typically informs how interior space is discussed, analysed and conceived. This is often reflected in the scope and ambition of the project. The resultant design proposal often seeks to form a 'symbiotic' or harmonious relationship whereby a careful contextual 'reading' of the site (through a site analysis) will suggest a way forward.

This initial architectural response develops through complex planning that considers the adaption of the existing (or new) space through the placement of newly created partitions, openings or voids as well as any bespoke interior fixtures. The scheme is developed to be sympathetic to the user and its new function. Detailed decisions regarding materials, furniture, lighting and graphics, especially how they will be 'read' against the shell of the building, still need to be made. Architecturally 'hard' materials such as timber, veneers, glass, steel and stone are more

prevalent in this type of interior but, as ever, there are always overlaps with the softer materials of the decorator. This process is supported by detailed project management and the production of a series of 'working drawings' (also important to the commercial sector) that aim to explain to the contractor the detail and technical aspects of the scheme. The regulatory aspects of the built environment need to be adhered to, as does the gaining of the relevant advice and/or permissions for any proposed structural alterations to the building shell. A subset of interior architecture is 'adaptive reuse', an approach that considers how an existing building (often historic) can be 'remodelled', usually as a result of a change of use. Interior architects generally pay more attention to the 'original life' and the resultant 'revitalization' of the existing building or site.

Interior design and the interior designer

As an interior designer you can choose to work either in the residential or commercial sphere; you can, of course, operate in both simultaneously. Interior designers undertaking residential work can ordinarily proffer more than the decorator by delving beneath the decorative surface to reconsider both space and its usage. As creative problem solvers they can rethink space and help to resolve any existing site problems. In contrast to this, the commercial (or trade) interior designer specializes in 'public' space, typically the interiors you enter when you leave your house to go about your daily life. Restaurants, bars, offices, retail, exhibition, healthcare and leisure spaces are all the preserve of the designer who chooses to specialize in the commercial sector. Commercial clients tend to be corporate and are often connected to the notion of a 'brand' and a brand message, so the commercial interior designer needs to deconstruct this brand to identify the prevailing ethos and the target customer in the search for a relevant design solution.

As a commercial designer you could find yourself working with a variety of site conditions; the design schemes are usually larger and more complex than those of the interior decorator, so the replanning of the existing space to house the new use is a priority. Spatial modifications can be proposed as part of this process but again only after consultation with the relevant professionals. Additionally, the interior designer has to understand the needs of the prospective user, whether they are the staff who work in the restaurant or the customer who eats there. User-centred design is a philosophy that prioritizes both an understanding of, and a dialogue with, the end user (for example, if you are working in healthcare or with a similarly vulnerable or unique user group), and it has become increasingly important within certain sectors. Graphics typically become an integral part of any commercial scheme, informing both the interior and exterior, aiming to create a cohesive look. Interior designers have the ability to think both decoratively and spatially, a combination of skills that helps them to address a project holistically.

Conclusion

Whether you see yourself as an interior decorator, an interior designer or interior architect, we are all creatives who work closely with clients to re-imagine an interior space for its new use and customer. The scale and ambition of the project might vary, but we are all concerned with taking a brief, developing a design response and getting the project built. The term 'interior designer' is useful because it can be seen as the one title that actually encompasses all of these definitions; it also serves to highlight how the work of the interior designer can be a rich mix of the architectural,

the commercial and the decorative. This realization suggests the use of 'interior designer' is relevant as a 'catch-all' or umbrella term, and it is used as such within this book.

On a final note, all design projects eventually have to consider the role of 'interior specification' – the use of colour, light, materials, furniture and fixtures in the development and completion of an interior scheme. All interior designers at some point have to ask themselves: what will the interior look like, what is the intended atmosphere, what will it feel like and what will I use to create this? This is one of the main focuses of this book.

Scope of this book – interior design and mise-en-scène

This book aims to illustrate how a decorative approach explored through the notion of an interior mise-en-scène can create a rich and meaningful space. The intention is to illustrate how this theoretical proposition, which is linked to an exploration of the physicality and psychology of staged space, can enhance current thinking relating to the decorated interior. Initially you might think that there is superficiality in employing such a cinematic approach, but the application of this theory quickly moves beyond a purely visual interpretation of the interior, to one that places the user experience at its heart.

Any history or discussion of interior design will reveal the polarity between the decorative and the architectural; this is by no means a new dilemma or debate. Over time the decorative has become unjustly maligned, driven partly by the desire of the interior designer to differentiate the scope of their work from that of the decorator. But surely the decorative is worth analysing and studying alongside the architectural to see what it offers to interior design as a discipline. This suggests that interior decoration is in dire need of, and would benefit from, a makeover of its very own.

Book structure

The contents of the chapters contained in this book are succinctly detailed below. The intention is to give the reader a concise overview of each chapter whilst highlighting the layout. The vast majority of these chapters will be supported by a series of case studies that aim to illustrate contextually the ingredients that form an interior mise-en-scène. The examples of interior mise-en-scène are deliberately far-ranging, drawing on the work of interior decorators and stylists, designers, the world of film and art, as well as encompassing that of architects who display an interior interest. Hopefully, this will convey a sense of its usefulness as a technique for considering interior space. The selection is determined by the need to illustrate and apply the principles of mise-en-scène to an understanding of interior decoration, rethought as staged space. As the project has developed, there has been a clear decision to concentrate on specific rooms and their individual mise-en-scène, much in the manner of a particular 'scene' from a film. For simplicity of structure, each case study within this book will always analyse interior space using three headings. Headings one and three will remain constant, whilst heading two will alter to reflect the emphasis of the particular chapter, typically:

The context – a concise background history; information that aims to set the scene.

The use of the interior setting, [or] of interior props, [or] of special effects, [or] of light and shadow, [or] the use of colour.

The narrative – analysis of the 'story' or possible 'perceptions' of the space for the audience or user.

The chapters will contain the following information:

Chapter One sets the scene regarding the interior design profession, whilst introducing 'staged space' and 'atmosphere' as central components of any discussion regarding mise-en-scène.

Chapter Two will explore the definition and theory of mise-en-scène through film that aims to instigate an alternative theoretical reading of the interior. In addition, the key ingredients of an interior mise-en-scène will be highlighted through the role setting, props and narrative play in the creation of this type of staged space.

Chapter Three will develop the notion of the interior 'setting' through an analysis of the decorative 'skin' of the space, essentially an interior's 'backdrop' or scenery. By placing the emphasis upon the skin of the interior, its narrative qualities will be explored through the story of its materiality.

Chapter Four will examine the role of the interior 'prop' through the use of accessories, furniture, fixtures and equipment.

Chapter Five will introduce interior 'special effects' by considering different perceptions of space through illusory, sensory and experiential readings of the interior.

Chapter Six will examine interior atmosphere through its use of light (both natural and artificial) as well as its accompanying shadow.

Chapter Seven will explore the application of colour, pattern, and graphics and its impact upon the perception of interior space.

What is staged space?

In essence, staged space is concerned with the assemblage of key interior ingredients that work together to holistically construct a specific scene.

The term 'staged space' has already been mentioned in the opening pages of this book and this would benefit from further explanation as the creation of a film's setting, conceived as a literal stage set, is central to the concept of the interior mise-en-scène. It is by its nature 'temporary', uses devices that can be removed or quickly altered, with a built-in shelf life. Staged space quickly transcends its physical setting through the arrangement of its 'setting', the interplay of 'props', the use of colour and materials, through to the application of light and shadow, all of which holistically combine to tell a story. This is, in essence, an interior 'assemblage' – elements that have been brought together or composed in the creation of a specific interior scene.

This is a description that would be familiar to any production designer working in film (or the theatre) as they are responsible, alongside the director and art department, for the creation of the sets and the development of a cohesive visual ambience. The French production designer and historian Léon Barsacq, in his comprehensive history of film design, eloquently makes the following statement:

Taken in its broadest sense, the film set is a discrete but ever-present character, the director's most faithful accomplice. It is simply a question of finding for each film the setting best calculated to situate the action geographically, socially, and dramatically.[4]
([1970] 1976: 122)

This concept of staged space embraces the premise of 'character' and aims to use the interior's artificially derived personality, through the ingredients previously mentioned, to create and enhance atmosphere. With the introduction of character this definition serves as a precursor to the notion of an interior mise-en-scène, and this description will be developed more fully in the next chapter.

What is atmosphere?

atmosphere

Line breaks: at¦mos|phere

Pronunciation: /ˈatməsfɪə

The pervading tone or mood of a place, situation, or creative work: the hotel has won commendations for its friendly, welcoming atmosphere.[5]
(Oxford Dictionaries, n.d.)

The above definition creates a useful starting point in any discussion of the decorated interior, as an initial understanding of the decorative lies in its ability to create and convey a carefully considered mood, one that is constrained by the building container. We all enjoy being immersed in the 'world' described and defined by an interior, but what forms this world and what is meant by the term 'atmosphere'?

1. Styled space and the creation of atmosphere

For many, the interior decorator is employed to create a mood because they have the visual flair and vision to pull a cohesive look together. How this mood is created is central to their craft as a decorator. Interior decorators examine every aspect of a room in the creation of a carefully constructed, pervasive interior atmosphere. This requires them to consider how the space is used, the overall feel or 'setting' of the interior, through to small details such as ornaments or props that are used to 'style' and accessorize. For many of the iconic decorators from the early to mid-twentieth century, the decorated interior was connected to a look you had created or developed and became synonymous with, for example, the 'Draper Touch' or the 'de Wolfe style'. It was all a matter of taste and they saw themselves as taste-makers. Whether you see yourself as bohemian, minimal or kitsch, there was a style or an aesthetic choice available to express yourself through your interior as, chameleon-like, it could don a thousand disguises.

Decorated style evolved from one of applied, historically derived, surface treatment or ornamentation, to one that prized individuality in the creation of an interior. Walter Benjamin's tome *The Arcades Project*, published posthumously, defined the 'physiognomy' of the nineteenth-century domestic interior as a place of bourgeois self-expression through its collection of objects. Its soft upholstered underbelly reveals the 'traces of the inhabitant'[6] ([1982] 2002: 20), whilst 'the space disguises itself – puts on, like an alluring creature, the costume of moods'[7] (ibid.: 216). The interior quickly became the location for self-expression, for display; it reflected its inhabitants, their rituals of the everyday.

The previous definition probably corresponds to what the majority of us think of as decorated atmosphere, in other words, a 'styled' space. But there is also the sense that the interior can convey an impression of its inhabitants, a personality created and defined by the user rather than one superimposed by a decorator. The next section sets out to expand this definition and represents an eclectic range of influences, brought together, because of their relation to the term 'atmosphere'.

2. Atmosphere and the sensory

The novelist Jun'ichirō Tanizaki in his seminal book *In Praise of Shadows*, first published in 1933, writes eloquently on the subject of beauty, especially a traditional Japanese allurement that immerses itself in the oriental dark, in its 'uncanny silence'[8] ([1933] 1977: 20). He likens a traditional Japanese interior to 'an ink wash painting'[9] (ibid.: 20) through its nuanced use of light and shade. A description of a rather prosaic everyday visit to an outdoor temple toilet, in his hands, becomes an evocative sensory experience:

As I have said there are certain prerequisites: a degree of dimness, absolute cleanliness, and quiet so complete one can hear the hum of a mosquito. I love to listen from such a toilet to the sound of softly falling rain, especially if this is a toilet of the Kantō region, with its long, narrow windows at floor level; there one can listen with such a sense of intimacy to the raindrops falling from the eaves and the trees, seeping into the earth as they wash over the base of a stone lantern and freshen the moss about the stepping stones.[10]

(ibid.: 04)

This alternative reading of atmosphere highlights its meteorological origins and proffers an interpretation centred on a climatic rendering of space. Linked to landscape through, say, the interplay of mist and light on a body of water, this concentrates upon the intangible qualities of space. Tanizaki's writings clearly favour a similar understanding of atmosphere in the creation of a mood, but they also suggest we 'experience' atmosphere as phenomenon through the qualities of light and dark, of sound or silence, of smell, of texture. The architectural theorist Pallasmaa's writings follow a similar theme, especially through his book *The Eyes of the Skin*. Pallasmaa laments the dominance of the visual sense that, for him, has resulted in a form of 'architectural autism'[11] (1996: 22). The French philosopher Michel Serres writes of the house as an 'orthopaedic sensorium'[12] (2008: 270), the interior composed of a series of 'linings' that become sensory wrappings for the body, whilst the award-winning architect Peter Zumthor also contributes to this sensory definition of atmosphere. For Zumthor, atmosphere is about an immersive experience of the senses, expressed as the 'magic of the real world'[13] ([2006] 2015: 19). This suggests that atmosphere is something we inhabit; we experience it through our bodily engagement with the world around us.

3. Atmosphere and the psychological

Whilst the modernists prized the rational architectural interior, the work of Freud and other psychoanalysts disrupted this unified vision with one of subjectivity. Much more than just a physical exploration of the house architecturally, Gaston Bachelard's writings prioritize the psychological. Originally published in 1958, through his book *The Poetics of Space*, the home becomes laden with metaphorical meaning and symbolism. Bachelard's 'oneiric' house is the house of psychology, of psychoanalysis, of the imagination. It has been formed by both our dreams and our nightmares. Bachelard theorizes that the 'imagination augments the values of reality'[14] ([1958] 1992: 03); for him, any understanding of atmosphere is connected to how we 'inhabit' and 'dwell' in a space. It is about the hidden or repressed meaning of the home, its symbolic connotations, and how this informs our understanding of a space and its atmosphere.

We can all recognize the pervasive symbolism of the hearth, or of the kitchen as the metaphorical 'heart' of the house, of the dark, dank, unchartered territory of the basement and its nightmare associations superbly exploited by countless horror films. The German philosopher Gernot Böhme proposes atmosphere as a new concept of aesthetics linked to perception, whilst his term 'tuned spaces'[15] (2013) resonates. He views atmosphere as capable of 'unify(ing) a diversity of impressions in a single emotive state'[16] (ibid.). Tonino Griffero shares Böhme's interest and he discusses atmosphere as 'spatialised feeling'[17] ([2010] 2014: 06), a 'quasi-thing' linked to a specific external situation that reverberates emotionally. All of these interpretations of atmosphere prioritize the psychological and introduce the imagination as an active participant in our perception of a particular place. Deep-seated, culturally ingrained ideas of privacy, of comfort, of gender and family also surface to colour our view of space. Pallasmaa sums this up beautifully by stating that we both 'remember' and 'imagine' places and it is these two intertwined systems that inform our understanding of 'lived space':

We live in worlds in which the material and the mental, the experienced, remembered, and imagined completely fuse into each other.[18] (2005: 129)

Conclusion

It is far too easy when teaching, thinking about and studying interior design to concentrate upon the 'visual' aspects of space. We are all drawn to images on the Internet, in magazines and published interior monographs, but any understanding of the interior needs to move beyond this visual fixation. The spatial, material and architectural qualities of space should all be considered, but this analysis should place at its heart the experiential qualities of the interior, in other words, what is it like to actually be in? This is a phenomenological reading that prioritizes the 'subjective' experience of space through perceptions and emotions, the sensory and the psychological. An interior's ability through its atmosphere and the staging of its space to tug at our imagination and emotions is an integral aspect of its impact upon our lives as the inhabitants of that space.

So what is atmosphere and how does it relate to the study of interior design? If an early definition or premise was that atmosphere was the 'pervading tone or mood of a place', is this simple definition still relevant? If the answer is no, then what has it become? The following four points aim to redefine interior atmosphere within the context of this book as:

1. Atmosphere is concerned with the visual look, character or prevailing mood of a place.
2. Atmosphere is also concerned with how we perceive and respond to space through its narrative, or story, in essence how it communicates. This should be considered as an integral part of the design process.
3. Atmosphere is also about the sensory experience – this is more than a visual reading, it is about our bodily involvement of being in and actively engaging with interior space. This means that we do not just see space, instead we hear, smell, taste and touch it, which should be given equal billing alongside the visual.
4. Finally, atmosphere is also about the psychological – this is concerned with the perceived emotional characteristics of a particular place. This approach deliberately exploits conventions or accepted norms to influence our perception of an interior space. It is about how a space feels, how it emanates a certain aura.

These four concluding points all suggest that atmosphere is not something that is just seen, it is a phenomenon – we sense, inhabit and even imagine aspects of it as part of an ongoing process of revelation. For the interior designer, atmosphere is artificially achieved, it is unapologetically man-made, which is why the term 'staged space' is useful as this historically suggests a consciously contrived theatricality. This conclusion requires a rethinking of atmosphere that moves beyond a purely styled response to one that embraces equally the decorative, narrative, sensory and psychological components of interior design.

FURTHER READING – EXPLORING ATMOSPHERE

The following books are all useful in helping the reader to explore further the main chapter theme pertaining to the re-evaluation of interior atmosphere. This approach is based on a transition, one that questions the stereotypical interpretation of atmosphere as something that is formed and described by styled space, to one that is balanced by its sensory articulation. This is further questioned through an understanding of its inherent psychological undertones.

The Poetics of Space (1958, with the first English translation in1964) by French philosopher Gaston Bachelard justifiably earns its place on any interior design book list as a seminal publication. Bachelard's text considers the psychology of the home through a discussion of the phenomenological term to 'dwell'. This book remains a useful vehicle for introducing interior space through the archetypal imagery that populates our subconscious.

The Eyes of the Skin: Architecture and the Senses (1996) by Finnish architect and architectural theorist Juhani Pallasmaa famously prioritizes a sensory re-evaluation of the experiential qualities of the built environment. Pallasmaa's argument centres on a critique of current architectural practice that, for him, displays a form of 'architectural autism', an approach that prioritizes the sense of sight whilst suppressing alternative sensory readings of space.

Atmospheres: Architectural Environments, Surrounding Objects (originally published in 2006) by award-winning Swiss architect Peter Zumthor beautifully outlines his stance regarding architectural atmosphere. For Zumthor, building is about capturing a certain mood, a magical, almost intangible quality that he explores through the 'poetics' of architecture as a space of sensory richness.

2 What's in a room?

The principles of mise-en-scène

Mise-en-scène therefore encompasses both what the audience can see and the way in which they are invited to see it. It refers to many of the major elements of communication in the cinema, and the combinations through which they operate expressively.[1]

(Gibbs, 2002: 05)

Figure 2.1
The Actress stage set, 1928. Canadian actress Norma Shearer on the set of The Actress (aka Trelawney of the Wells), directed by Sidney Franklin.
What does an interior become when it explores theoretically the concept of mise-en-scène?

The power of the interior

An interior can become more than a carefully constructed mood. Interiors relate to our lives and can become living, breathing, ever-changing representations of us as individuals, companies or brands. An interior can act as a mirror, reflecting the lives of the occupants it contains, or it can concentrate on communicating the message of a corporate brand. It has social, psychological and cultural connotations. The interior can represent the ad hoc, the cluttered traces of everyday life, or the 'uber' designed, carefully staged 'inner life of a building'. At its best, an interior can proffer a pervasive atmosphere that tugs on our heartstrings, quickens our senses, pulls at our emotions and packs a psychological punch. The power of the interior can be harnessed and used to particular effect. Interiors can wrap around us, they can be immersive, they can tell a story, or they can help stage an experience. This leads to the questions: what does this type of interior look like and what are the components that help to form it? To answer these questions, a discussion of both film and mise-en-scène will be useful at this stage; these questions have helped to frame the focus for this chapter. It is:

CHAPTER FOCUS

- An introduction to the term 'mise-en-scène'.
- An exploration of mise-en-scène in relation to interior design.
- The development of an understanding of the typical interior elements or 'ingredients' that form an interior mise-en-scène.

What is mise-en-scène?

Mise-en-scène is essentially the art of 'presenting' – by this means, it successfully projects an 'expressive' visual coherence to its audience.

Interiors surround us in the real world of the everyday as well as the illusory world of film. We all unknowingly absorb these visual stimuli on a daily basis as we enter a series of built interiors whilst going about our daily lives. Our leisure time is spent entering spaces of the imagination through books and, digitally, through the world of film, television and virtual gaming. All of these spaces – real or imaginary – can shape our view of the world as interior designers. It is an obvious leap but why can we not be inspired by all forms and expressions of the interior?

Films create a world whose setting is completely illusory. Every facet has been designed to create a location for the main characters and to tell the story cinematically. This setting quickly transcends its physical limitations to help frame 'expressively' how we as the audience read, understand and emotionally respond to the story being told. A key aspect of this storytelling is mise-en-scène, which literally translates as 'putting into the scene'. This term originated in the theatre and traditionally refers to all the visual elements that were used to 'stage' a production:

As you would expect from the term's theatrical origins, mise-en-scène includes those aspects of film that overlap with the art of the theater [*sic*]: setting, lighting, costume, and behaviour of the figures. In controlling the mise-en-scène, the director stages the event for the camera.[2]

(Bordwell and Thompson, [1979] 2001: 156)

Interestingly, these origins highlight how mise-en-scène has managed to cross theatrical and cinematic boundaries, whilst operating in both simultaneously. It has taken the ingredients that helped to stage a production for a theatrical audience and initially transposed these in front of the camera. With the arrival of cinema, a new component is added into the mix – the camera, and the camera lens is used to 'frame' and 'taint' the action further, replacing the proscenium arch and curtains of the stage. Regardless of the context, the common denominator has always been how the audience is presented with a carefully orchestrated and staged 'scene' or 'shot'.

Mise-en-scène – a definition

Cinema, in borrowing this term, has extended its usage, naturally including other devices that help to form this cohesive first impression. Gibbs' analysis[3] (2002: 06–26) is comprehensive; he cites nine ingredients that all work together in the creation of mise-en-scène, whilst Bordwell and Thompson[4] ([1979] 2001: 158–174) mention just four. The term remains loose in its definition, even fluid, as elements seem to be added and subtracted at will, but essentially comprises the position, movement and technical possibilities of the camera; the composition and design of the set; the placement of the props and actors; their relation to each other; and the setting. How the actors are dressed and how they perform, how the whole scene is then lit and framed are central to a film's mise-en-scène. Martin[5] (2014: 16) goes further – even advocating editing as having an impact upon an audience's appreciation of the term. Whilst it is useful to know and list the individual ingredients, it has always been their interrelationship that produces the overall effect.

Within film theory, the term has had its detractors and it has been criticized equally for its reduction of film to its 'style', or for overemphasizing and celebrating the notion of the film director as 'auteur'. Criticism aside, it does raise interesting questions regarding the relationship between meanings and the look or 'style' of a film that suggests an affiliation to interior design. This realization brings us quickly into the realm of production design, and production designers work alongside the director to coordinate the visual coherence of cinematic space. They marry the film's screenplay to a manufactured set or adapted location, bringing that vision to life through the coordination of the art department. As Ettedgui states in his introduction to the discipline: 'we can define the role of the production designer as being the architect of the illusions depicted on the screen'[6] (1999: 10), but mise-en-scène is about more than just the reality or tangibility of a set. In films and spaces of the imagination, interiors and buildings become settings that have psychological meaning; they act as metaphors for the character or the story to create visually complex atmospheres and pictorial interpretations. This constructed mise-en-scène, one of staged space, communicates the film's intended sense of time and space as required for the story through the design of a 'physical' setting or environment. This setting is then enhanced through the use of elements that enrich the mood of the film 'psychologically'. These two elements together create a rich atmosphere – a mix of the physical or actual, the psychological or interpreted. Both contribute to the mise-en-scène and how the story is told.

Schaal's essay exploring cinematic spaces of the psyche[7] (2000: 12–15) reinforces this view of filmic space as one laden with psychological meaning. Pallasmaa in his exploration of the existential space of cinema makes a strong case for what he calls the 'mental states' of cinematic space as 'amplifiers of specific emotions'[8] (2007: 07). Meanwhile, Cairns, in his analysis of the visual language of cinema, highlights two opposing factors – physical space versus cinematographic space[9] (2013: 163). The former relates to the physical set whilst the latter details how that physicality is altered through the perceptual medium of cinema, a stance that clearly correlates to the concept of mise-en-scène. Martin refers to this as the 'transformative' aspect of the term:

Mise-en-scène can transform the elements of a given scene; it can transform a narrative's destination; it can transform our mood or our understanding as we experience the film.[10]

(2014: 19–20)

Mise-en-scène and film

It is always useful to contextualize a theory. To help explore the concept of mise-en-scène further, some examples of iconic films and their justifiably famous interiors are included below. At this stage these descriptions are intended as brief forays only, something to help set the scene, as it were. They do, however, begin to suggest interior ingredients that will be discussed comprehensively in later chapters.

The mise-en-scène for *The Cabinet of Dr. Caligari*, 1919, directed by Robert Wiene, is influential because of its interpretation of German expressionism cinematically, a movement that sought to express emotions spatially and artistically. The film was shot on a closed sound stage, using sets that were geometrically distorted, deliberately claustrophobic, and exaggerated by painted light and shadow. Its mise-en-scène aimed to illustrate the villain's delusions and his 'reign of terror'[11] (LoBrutto, 2002: 95). The framing of the film through its expressionistic scenography created interior spaces that aimed to pictorially imply emotional states, and it is this symbiosis of the emotional to the inner world of the interior that makes this example so interesting within the context of this book. Because of its relevance this case study will be explored in more detail in the next chapter.

For anyone interested in the study of interiors, the work of American film director Wes Anderson emanates an irresistible draw. His cinematic environments, because of their sectional 'dollhouse' quality and their 'planimetric staging'[12] (Bordwell, 2015: 238) immortalize the interior as a recurring motif or habitual presence. These visual compositions neatly 'frame' the film's characters within their fictional backdrops, spatial situations that always capture through their setting and props the idiosyncrasies of their invented personalities. Typical of this approach is *The Grand Budapest Hotel*, released in 2014. Anderson, alongside production designer Adam Stockhausen, never attempts to create a historically accurate, grand, European hotel as the setting for the story. Instead, he imagines a brightly coloured, hyper-real space that mimics its architectural predecessors through an evocative use of 'romantic realism'[13] (Boone, 2015: 143) via inserted and layered sets into found locations.

Another iconic cinematic example is the mise-en-scène for Miss Haversham in David Lean's *Great Expectations*, released in 1946, with the sets designed by John Bryan. Miss Haversham, the embittered jilted bride, is surely one of Charles Dickens' most famous creations. The interior setting she occupies, that of the abandoned wedding feast engulfed by shadow and decay, symbolically implies 'a living fossil, whose room is frozen at the moment of her interrupted wedding'[14] (Brownlow, 1996: Figure 13). This is beautifully

Figure 2.2
***The Cabinet of Dr. Caligari*, 1919, director Robert Wiene.**
The iconic mise-en-scène for *The Cabinet of Dr. Caligari* was created by using painted, geometrically distorted light and shadow that aimed to convey emotions through the staging of its space.

illustrated by cobwebbed props, complemented by extreme contrasts of light and shadow that capture this bridal relic replete in her tattered wedding gown. The design of the interior clearly strives to represent its famous fictional resident and this film set introduces the notion of how a character's psychosis can be used to inform interior space.

What is narrative?

Any discussion of mise-en-scène needs to consider narrative. The cinematic examples just discussed illustrate how mise-en-scène is used spatially as a mnemonic device, a device that expressively conveys meaning through interior characterization. This characterization is integral to the narrative, supporting and underlining the story. It seems an obvious starting point but narrative in its most literal sense appears as a 'story' being told. The history of storytelling goes back to time immemorial, and has grown through the art of oration and the individual storyteller, the travelling theatre troupe, on the theatre stage and, finally, through the films and books of today. This narrative tradition has transferred

Figure 2.3
***The Grand Budapest Hotel**,* 2014, featuring Paul Schlase, Tony Revolori, Tilda Swinton, Ralph Fiennes, and directed by Wes Anderson. Anderson's highly stylized and idiosyncratic mise-en-scène uses costumes, colour, framing and composition to capture the personalities that people his films. These characteristics are then transferred into the interior setting.

into the world of the interior with many spaces intentionally telling a story. But narrative can be interpreted beyond a straightforward plot – it can also communicate an idea, or reveal an essential essence to its intended audience.

The next section aims to explore these ideas contextually through specific examples of historic interiors that display the traits of mise-en-scène. Clearly, narrative can give meaning to an interior, and is central to the concept of an interior mise-en-scène, perhaps because the interior is itself inherently illusory. It can 'reveal' its true nature, the bricks and mortar that form its bones, the exposed plaster of its bare skin, or it can pretend to be something else. By evoking a certain quality, cloaking its true essence, the interior moves

into the realm of decorative storytelling, that of an interior mise-en-scène.

What is an interior mise-en-scène?

A set must take into account one other factor: the psychology and behaviour of those intended to inhabit it. If it is successful, the set will replace with its mere appearance a whole page of description in a novel and verbal descriptions that would be boring on film. Robert Mallet-Stevens, who was one of the first to study seriously the role of the set in a film, wrote, 'A film set, in order to be a good set, must act. Whether realistic or expressionist, modern or ancient, it must play its part'.[15]

(Barsacq, [1970] 1976: 125)

2.4

Figure 2.4
Great Expectations, **1946, director David Lean.**
Famously, Satis House with its gothic mise-en-scène, the lair of Miss Haversham from *Great Expectations*, captures the abandoned wedding breakfast cinematically. Miss Haversham is literally fossilized within its four walls.

It is clear that a borrowing of some of the ideas from film and production design, as just described, can enhance our understanding of interior atmosphere, and suggest another way of thinking about the decorated interior as one of staged space. Integral to this investigation is the reworking of the elements of the mise-en-scène to those that are more attuned to the study of interior design.

The obvious difference between theatrical and cinematic concepts of mise-en-scène has to be the presence of the camera. This study does not set out to explore in detail the mechanics and technique of the camera, or the art of post-production (this would be an altogether-different book), although these aspects will certainly be referenced where relevant. Instead, it will naturally focus on those elements that overlap with the ingredients of an interior mise-en-scène. Through an embracing of the decorative, this study will instead focus on the perceptual impression of staged space through its perceived character or atmosphere, alongside the recurring ingredients that bring it to life.

Interior mise-en-scène – a definition

An interior mise-en-scène encompasses the physical, the psychological and the narrative properties of space in the harnessing of an immersive atmosphere that aims to 'taint' an audience's perception of any given space.

In essence, an interior mise-en-scène takes as its starting point the physicality of the theatre set and marries it to filmic ideas relating to perception and meaning. Bearing this in mind, a working definition for an interior mise-en-scène has become characterized by three key elements – the physical, the psychological and the narrative – and these are examined in detail.

- **The physical mise-en-scène** is concerned with the design or staging of the physical environment or 'setting' alongside the selection of the 'props' it will contain. Typically, this would include decisions on the final 'form' of the space as well as its 'decorative' style. The choice of props, typically furniture, accessories, fixtures and equipment, completes this scene.
  Typical interior elements – it is all about the final arrangement, shape and finish of the walls, floor and ceiling that form the setting, and how this can be enhanced by the use of interior props. The setting considers more than just the surface decoration because the arrangement of the horizontal and vertical surfaces, the 'skin' of the setting, can be manipulated both spatially and volumetrically.

- **The psychological mise-en-scène** includes elements that work with the setting and props, as outlined above, and aims to enhance a specific 'mood', whilst at the same time hoping to elicit an emotional response by influencing our perception of space.
  Typical interior elements – this is concerned with how the use of light, shadow, colour, scale, composition and even special effects are employed for dramatic effect. It is also concerned with our sensory engagement and psychological perception of space. As mentioned in the previous chapter, this approach deliberately exploits conventions or accepted norms to subtly influence our reading of an interior.

- **The narrative mise-en-scène** – the elements already described work together to create an experiential interior atmosphere of staged space. This is about an immersive environment that tells a 'story' through an unfolding narrative that cajoles, evokes and even deceives to reveal a certain quality or mood. The role of symbolism, metaphor or motif can be of great importance to this form of interior storytelling, whilst visual, psychological and sensory tricks are used to great effect.

This book aims to explain how these elements all contribute to the creation of interior atmosphere, by illustrating how they can be used to develop your thinking. This is a highly personal interpretation of mise-en-scène, and its application to the study of interiors has been honed through years of teaching. The inspirational starting point of the filmed interior and staged space has been adapted in its application to the world of interior design. I hope you will forgive these liberties. The elements or ingredients that remain can be worked together in the creation of a mise-en-scène for the interior. This definition has proved invaluable over the years for its ability to develop thinking beyond the current rather-restricted perception that relates to interior decoration. It gleefully combines a love of the cinema with a love of interior design and this book has evolved out of this teaching experience.

Revealing interior mise-en-scène, an alternative view of interior design

All the world's a stage, and all the men and women merely players.[16]

(William Shakespeare, *As You Like It*, Act II, Scene VII, [1599–1600] 1963: 77)

So how did we get to this point? To help contextualize these ideas, a thematic collection of interiors that evidence the ingredients and preoccupations of interior mise-en-scène will be highlighted. This selection simply categorizes, according to the recurring traits that are common to this genre, traits that have already been identified. The 'physical' and 'psychological' ingredients alongside 'narrative' can now be employed as a device to track interiors that display this bias. With this in mind, the past can be revisited, essentially pillaged, in the search for examples that evidence these concerns. For the purposes of coherency, this interior collation has to deliberately cross decorative, design and architectural boundaries in acknowledgement of the many facets and practitioners, all from a wealth of different backgrounds, that have helped to form and mould the discipline that we know today as interior design. In discussing the decorated interior, it is no coincidence that the French word 'décor' has dual meaning and translates as both stage scenery and interior decoration[17] (Rugoff, 2010: 11). This duality serves to underline the link between cinematic interpretations of space, the theatricality of the film setting, staged space and certain aspects of the interior.

This alternative view of interior design loosely echoes the birth and evolution of film (apart from one notable exception) in its selection of interiors that historically and temporally correspond to this era. This felt appropriate given that the devices most commonly associated with cinematic expressions of space increased exponentially with the advent of the big screen. However, there is by necessity, as has already been noted, an overlap with theatrical staging, as early film sets echoed their theatrical counterparts in their reworking of the scenic backdrop and props into one of staged space. The Lumière brothers' first films from 1895, developed through their patented film camera, simply recorded everyday scenes, whereas it is the influential Georges Méliès (1861–1938), as the pioneer of the film set, who strikes a chord with the notion of interior mise-en-scène already outlined in this book. Méliès created fantastic interior environments that borrowed heavily from theatrical staging (he was, after all, the proud owner of a theatre and a keen fan of magical illusion), whilst simultaneously developing celluloid optical trickery.

Theatrical scenery is inevitably a fixed point, a 'tableau' that plays to its audience by using a combination of painted scenography, props, lighting, acoustics, costumes and special effects to evocatively set the scene. Early film sets paralleled this theatrical tradition alongside a keen interest in artifice and illusion. As film evolved, the camera became more

2.5

Figure 2.5
Film still from Georges Méliès *Le Voyage Dans la Lune* (*A Trip to the Moon*), 1902.
Méliès pioneered the use of the closed film set employing props, painted backdrops and traditional theatrical special effects, whilst simultaneously developing cinematic optical illusions in the creation of fantastic environments for the big screen.

mobile – no longer just recording a fixed scene. An increased desire for realism, echoed by the shifting of production from the introverted world of the closed set in favour of location work, inevitably transferred this focus. It is the former description, that of an artificially enhanced interior reality, that corresponds directly with the notion of an interior mise-en-scène. Through the lens of the camera, interior space becomes rethought as a scenic backdrop complete with props that can be charged with a preordained meaning. Additionally, narrative, interior spectacle and notions of the user as willing actor or audience become recurring motifs.

Bearing all of this in mind, Le Corbusier's (1887–1965) design for the rooftop Parisian Apartment (1929–31) of Carlos de Beistegui (a famous collector and *bon vivant*) sets the scene for an exemplary example of this type of staged space. The apartment utilizes Le Corbusier's famous 'architectural promenade' as a route through space. This route cleverly shifts the focus from one of introversion to extroversion, whilst simultaneously embracing sensory and acoustic spatial difference as a sequential series of indoor to outdoor spaces, envisioned as carefully staged scenes and framed views. This interior embraced spatial special effects such as mechanized walls, a retractable chandelier and the *pièce de résistance* – motorized clipped hedges that shifted to reveal carefully selected urban tableaux. The whole experience was offset by the incongruous use of domestic props such as a fireplace surreally juxtaposed against a manicured lawn and the metropolitan backdrop.

**Figure 2.6
Beistegui Apartment, Paris, France, 1929–31, by Le Corbusier, decorative scheme by Carlos de Beistegui and Emilio Terry.** This example of staged space utilizes differing spaces, motorized hedges and framed city views as scenic backdrops alongside incongruously positioned domestic props to evoke a surrealistic mise-en-scène.

2.6

The now-legendary 'Phantasy Landscape' for the Visiona II Exhibition in 1970, developed by Verner Panton (1926–98), clearly stages space using the ingredients of mise-en-scène. The space (in reality, a futuristic rethinking of the domestic realm) offered different opportunities to relax within an extraordinary interior environment. The surface of the interior became a three-dimensional, tactile, contoured world that invited repose. This interior psychologically captured the sixties' zeitgeist of 'The Happening' as a staged event by creating an immersive haptic adventure that combined colour, material, light and even sound to overwhelm the senses. Both these examples through their interplay of setting, props, light and framed views resonate with mise-en-scène and staged space whilst prioritizing the sensory experience of space.

The work of French designer Philippe Starck alongside property developer Ian Schrager also chimes with this notion of mise-en-scène as they prioritized the concept of a man-made interior spectacle. Their raising of the hotel to a unique boutique experience in the 1980s and 1990s was the antithesis of the international brand mediocrity that prevailed at the time. The hotel lobby became the location for the 'staging' of everyday life, repackaged as a carefully choreographed slice of urban life complete with 'actors' (in reality, willing guests), amidst iconic props and carefully manicured hotel staff. It is worth noting that this participatory audience becomes integral to the overall effect and their 'occupation' alongside the accompanying hubbub of a busy space adds another rich layer to interior atmosphere.

Figure 2.7
Visiona II Exhibition, Cologne, Germany, 1970, by designer Verner Panton. This reconstruction at the Danish Design Centre from 2003 reveals Panton's interior mise-en-scène ingredients of colour, light and surface. These are overlain with haptic and acoustic qualities to create a truly immersive sensory environment.

More literal interpretations of film through the artifice of the physical 'set' can be found in Colomina's analytical study of the houses designed by architect Adolf Loos (1870–1933). She theorizes Loos' concept of home as a 'spatial–psychological device'[18] ([1994] 1996: 238); in reality, an interior fixture expressed as a raised platform becomes a vantage point, a space of surveillance from which the inhabitant can both see and be partially seen. This 'theatre box' common to the Moller House, Vienna (1928) and the Müller House, Prague (1930) is about the introversion of the gaze as the interior becomes an inhabited stage. This reading clearly references the concerns of an interior mise-en-scène by acknowledging the psychological component of atmosphere.

A more disturbing interpretation of the stage set can be found in the 'Panopticon' conceived by social theorist Jeremy Bentham in the late eighteenth century. This institutional space, for him, formed the blueprint of a model prison, as spatially all the inmates could be observed by just one unseen

2.8

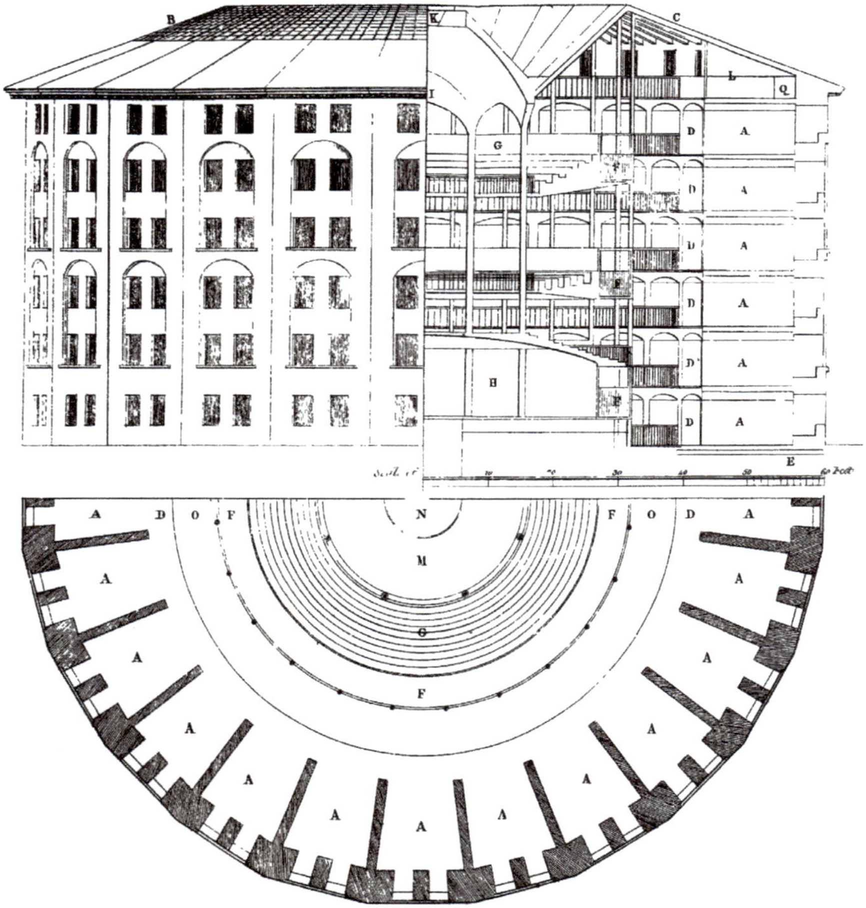

Figure 2.8
Design for a Panopticon Prison, 1843, by social theorist Jeremy Bentham.
Here, staged space becomes the ultimate expression of surveillance – a voyeuristic space of exposure through Foucault's reading of Bentham's social experiment.

observer. The design, circular in plan, located prisoners' cells on the perimeter, whilst positioning a watchtower in the centre. Openings ensured that the inmate could always be viewed: 'they are like so many cages, so many small theatres, in which each actor is alone, perfectly individualised and constantly visible'[19] (Foucault, [1975] 1991: 200). This pervasive use of surveillance forced the inmates, through the illusion of constant observation, to behave accordingly. The French philosopher Michel Foucault famously used the Panopticon as a metaphor for an all-encompassing community control, mirroring a shift in society from the 'exceptional discipline' of the individual prison cell to one of 'generalised surveillance' of society at large[20] (ibid.: 209). For Foucault, spatial transparency ironically becomes a societal trap as we are all exposed to the continual gaze of the omnipresent 'big brother'. These examples all conceptually re-imagine the set as a central preoccupation of staged space. This becomes a place of spectacle, characterized in this instance through the need to control, display, entice or impress. Interior space through this reading becomes the locus for a carefully staged voyeuristic production of revelation.

This next section concentrates on interiors that evidence narrative as a guiding design principle. For obvious reasons storytelling remains an integral aspect of any interior mise-en-scène as oral theatrical traditions were quickly translated to the big screen through the medium of film. Whilst the majority of films were guided by a script, the film's backdrop developed as a device that could reinforce this central narrative expressively. This approach recognizes the interior as a medium for storytelling, an inherently divinatory device that can display individually or collectively the interests, obsessions and preoccupations of its current resident. This highly personal rendering of space can be seen in Salvador Dalí's 'The Mae West Room', located in the Dalí Theatre and Museum in Figueres, Spain. Dalí (1904–89), as a surrealist artist, played with anthropomorphism by attributing human characteristics to a physical space. It is, in essence, an elaborate surrealist joke, a dual narrative expressed as a form of alchemy that takes mundane, everyday objects through a transformative process in the creation of an alternative reality. The surrealists famously re-evaluated the traditional meaning of objects through their oneiric preoccupations, whilst a recurring motif of the Dadaists and the art of Duchamp and his 'ready-mades' saw utilitarian objects taken out of context, become imbued with new meaning within a gallery setting.

This continual questioning of meaning can also be found in the work of Kurt Schwitters (1887–1948). His 'Merzbau' (built 1923–37, but eventually destroyed by an Allied bombing raid in 1943) remains hugely influential as it represented an immersive spatial environment, a piece of art that literally erupted from the canvas to invade parasitically his family home in Hanover, Germany. This artistic growth with architectural aspirations became a grotto of the extraordinary: in reality, an interior assemblage composed of incremental layers of plaster, refuse and re-purposed found objects. Spatially, this formed a series of personal shrines, each decorated with trophies and mementoes dedicated to a particular person, movement or event of personal significance to the artist. Through narrative, this interior captures the intent of a carefully constructed personal museum, a belief system borne out of one man's inner obsessions and working processes[21] (Gamard, 2000: 104). Both these examples are clearly precursors of Installation Art, an artistic movement that sought to create immersive spatial experiences rescaled from that of an object to a fully formed environment. This is an approach that clearly resonates with the design of interiors. Narrative, for these two artists, is clearly linked to an expression of self through a questioning of the quotidian, everyday functional aspect of the interior. This inner world instead becomes the province of the fantastic, and it is this continual interrogation that is central to an interior

mise-en-scène through its carefully crafted character and directed expression.

In contrast, British architect Nigel Coates' 'Caffe Bongo', built in Tokyo, Japan in 1986, embraces a thematic approach. This interior embodied his belief that narrative is integral to design. Inspired by Federico Fellini's iconic sixties' film *La Dolce Vita*, this themed interior uses carefully chosen interior props such as an aircraft wing, salvaged materials and classical statues to visually reference both the film and its Italian setting. Narrative within the context of the interior can, however, be expressed in a

Figure 2.9
'The Mae West Room', Dalí Theatre and Museum, 1974, Figueres, Spain by artist Salvador Dalí. This surreal mise-en-scène uses narrative through symbolism and metaphor to transform everyday items through dual meaning. Familiar domestic props, when viewed collectively, become the face of Hollywood actress Mae West, famous in the 1930s and 1940s.

2.10

Figures 2.10 and 2.11
Caffe Bongo, Tokyo, Japan, 1989, by architect Nigel Coates.
Caffe Bongo's mise-en-scène utilizes props developed from a 'bricolage' of European cultural references derived from a narrative that relates to director Federico Fellini's 1960 film *La Dolce Vita*.

2.11

myriad manner and the Brasserie restaurant in New York (2000) by Diller + Scofidio, now Diller, Scofidio + Renfro, is justly famous for its narrative of interior surveillance and voyeurism. Memorably, an entrance scenario for the prospective customer reinterprets the notion of the directed gaze of the other diners. A central preoccupation of their work is a questioning of 'display'[22] (Betsky, 2003: 560–1), an aspect of society that we all encounter on a daily basis, and this is in evidence here. Developed as a response to the restaurant's basement location at the bottom of Mies Van der Rohe's Seagram Tower, the lack of street view triggered a rethinking of exposure. Finally, mention must be made of Daniel Libeskind's Jewish Museum in Berlin, which was completed in 1999, built as a haunting paean to the lost Jewish

Figures 2.12 and 2.13
Brasserie, New York, USA, 2000, by Diller + Scofidio.
Diller + Scofidio's *oeuvre* evidences a preoccupation with display and this narrative is central to the staging and voyeuristic concept of this restaurant interior.

community and victims of the Holocaust. This building and its expressive interior masochistically displays a narrative of loss that is literally 'incised' onto its surface or 'cut' into its central voids. It incorporates spaces of silence, of emptiness, as well as areas that are left unheated and permeated to embrace the noise of the city in an interior that is alive to the possibilities of a psychological atmosphere. More than any other example, this seminal precedent helped to reignite the debate regarding meaning, emotion and the built environment.

This grouping of interiors with narrative aspirations highlights how this genre can explore both the performative and psychological aspects of the interior. Interiors that question the private and repackage it as public phenomenon (and vice versa) are legion, whilst interiors that expressively communicate past tragedies by wearing a mantel of grief through symbolic remembrance are not uncommon. Interiors can be rethought to emanate a certain character, whilst showmanship and spectacle have always been, and remain, a pervading component of this form of staged space. All of these preoccupations are translated expressively through the notion of an interior mise-en-scène.

Figures 2.14 and 2.15 Jewish Museum, Berlin, Germany, completed in 1999, by architect Daniel Libeskind. Libeskind's Jewish Museum explores a narrative of loss by using an architecture that resonates emotionally with meaning and is alive to the sensory and psychological possibilities of the built environment.

Conclusion

This initial attempt at defining traits common to the study of an interior mise-en-scène identified key physical and psychological ingredients alongside different interpretations of narrative as key design attributes. Subsequent chapters aim to expand this initial understanding of an interior mise-en-scène for the reader by analysing respectively the interior setting, the use of props, the impact of interior special effects, considerations of light and shadow, through to the application of colour. Common to all of these ingredients is how they can be combined to taint our view of space in the creation of a unified interior ambience or mise-en-scène. Central to this is our sensory and psychological awareness of this type of manufactured environment. The relationship these ingredients have to interior atmosphere will be examined and discussed at length. Böhme[23] (2013) would refer to these ingredients as 'generators' – elements that help to create atmosphere by 'setting the conditions'. As designers, we can select and employ interior ingredients and then compose them in the creation of habitable spaces. So, to borrow Böhme's terminology, the subsequent chapters identify generators of interior atmosphere that, within the context of this book, will be referred to as ingredients. Now it is just a case of mastering these mise-en-scène ingredients.

FURTHER READING – EXPLORING MISE-EN-SCÈNE

This chapter aimed to introduce the term mise-en-scène and use this as a vehicle for re-evaluating interior space. Details of the books that have been central to this thinking are included below as a further guide for the interested reader. Whilst mise-en-scène is useful theoretically as an analytical tool, it has a more purposeful role to the study of interiors, as it offers a ready-made set of ingredients that can be utilized in the creation of staged space and atmosphere.

Mise-En-Scène: Film Style and Interpretation (2002), by John Gibbs, succinctly explores mise-en-scène within the history of film. Gibbs usefully describes the individual components central to this cinematic approach, whilst contextualizing them through detailed film readings.

Léon Barsacq's *Caligari's Cabinet and other Grand Illusions, a History of Film Design* (1976) remains a useful book detailing the art of production design. As a veteran designer, Barsacq develops his theoretical stance of the stage set as an ever-present 'character', an approach that is central to an interior mise-en-scène.

The Art of the Stage Set as a Paradigm for an Aesthetics of Atmosphere (2013) by German philosopher Gernot Böhme is available online at: http://ambiances.revues.org/315. Böhme's paper posits atmosphere as something inherently intangible, almost meteorological in substance, that gains coherency through the art of theatre design. Böhme advocates the stage set as a master class in the creation of atmosphere. Böhme's extensive writings on atmosphere can also be found in *The Aesthetics of Atmosphere* (2017).

Finally, any of the films mentioned in this chapter (and all forthcoming chapters) are a great starting point for understanding mise-en-scène's application to the interior.

3 The interior setting

The backdrop or 'skin' of the space

What matters is that, in speaking of atmospheres, we refer to their character. With this term character we already bring our understanding of atmospheres close to the sphere of physiognomy and theatre. The character of an atmosphere is the way in which it communicates a feeling to us as participating subjects.[1]

(Böhme, 2013)

Figure 3.1
The famous miniature family theatre owned by Stanley Lupino, a well-known comedian, 1940.
This chapter will explore the role of the interior 'setting' conceived as a scenic backdrop, a physical 'skin' that can be endlessly manipulated and expressively transformed.

What is an interior setting?

The 'setting' forms the 'backdrop' to the interior, essentially the physical surfaces that create and enclose a room – its walls, floor and ceiling. This setting has an imprint of the atmospheric, aiming to communicate a certain aura through its form, materiality and finish. It helps to 'set the scene' or 'set the tone' for the interior by evoking a specific time or place, whilst its staging can enhance a particular effect. Decisions regarding its surface finish are often a matter of personal or cultural taste; fads come and go; and the interior moves with the times, regularly changing its setting to 'keep up with the Joneses'. Alternatively, it can eschew fashion and become something more serious, aiming to communicate a deeper, more controlled identity or meaning.

So if the setting is an ingredient common to all interiors, what can this typical, even archetypal, ingredient, found in even the most pedestrian of spaces, be coaxed to achieve? This chapter will explore the possibilities of the setting as a 'skin' that can be continually manipulated into a different life and aesthetic meaning. Bearing this in mind, the focus for this chapter is as follows:

CHAPTER FOCUS

- An introduction to the 'interior setting' or decorative backdrop within interior design.
- An exploration of design approaches that utilize the interior setting through the four categories of surface, layered, manipulated, and three-dimensional 'skin'.
- An investigation of the interior setting and its role in the creation of an interior mise-en-scène.

What is the physical environment – the skin?

What do you consider when you think of the skin of a decorated room – paint, wallpaper, textiles? This chapter represents a conscious attempt to deconstruct these typical ingredients and look at them afresh. Clearly, the skin forms the surface of the setting; it is the covering or surface treatment that it presents to the world. This skin is by nature malleable, easily influenced or shaped. It can be just a simple painted surface, or it can become layered, accruing wallpaper, textural or material coverings over time. It can be manipulated, teased into a variety of textural surfaces or low-relief mouldings; it can even liberate itself from the actual setting by forming three-dimensional ribbons, origami folds and facets, even spaces, thus taking on a life of its own, distinct from the original room confines. Bearing these possibilities in mind, the skin of an interior setting can be loosely grouped into four categories, all of which relate to their treatment, these are:

1. Surface skin;

2. Layered skin;

3. Manipulated skin;

4. Three-dimensional skin.

Each of these four categories reflects a conscious decision to highlight the properties of the skin that starts as a simple adhered surface and progresses to something increasingly spatial. These will be explored in more detail in the summary to follow and through the case studies in the latter half of this chapter.

Surface skin

Surface skin is primarily concerned with decisions relating to the immediate surface of the setting; it is often lightweight in nature and easy to apply or change. It typically, but not exclusively, ranges from a simple painted finish to the use of 'thin' decorative paper layers, such as wallpaper, through to the exposure of the original plaster setting, complete with its very own patina of age. A painted skin is perhaps the quickest and most cost-effective way of creating instant impact by changing the original surface to one that is full of colour or decorative painted pattern. Wallpaper differs

from the painted skin largely because it has more substance than paint, although the effect it produces can be similar. Supplied as a roll, this product becomes a lightweight layer that adheres to the original surface. The choice of finish is endless, ranging from simple colour, through pattern and graphics, to realistic digital imagery.

To illustrate this approach, an image of the remodelled interiors of the Birkbeck Centre for Film and Visual Media Research, London, designed by Surface Architects in 2007, is included. This interior showcases an approach to a surface skin that vividly uses coloured perspective distortions. These painted graphics

3.2

Figure 3.2
Birkbeck Centre for Film and Visual Media Research, London, England, 2007, by Surface Architects.
Surface skin – this example illustrates how colourful painted graphics can create a striking interior setting that contributes towards a strong visual identity, which resonates for a specific community of users.

extend from the walls and ceiling onto the resin floor as a series of 'cinematic snapshots' composed of contrasting colours and finishes. These frozen moments, akin to stop-frame animation, have literally become imprinted on the surface of the interior. Architect Richard Scott describes the project's generative process as 'it's not just architecture as image but architecture as moving image. So the cinema was actually designed through animations ... we actually used animation as a means of generating the design'[2] (cited in Metalworks/Surface Architects, 2007: 63). This conceptual approach to the decorative surface of the skin cleverly creates an interior that acknowledges the building's function and reverence for film in the creation of a suitable ambience.

As Birkbeck illustrates, narrative concerns can inform the design of interior space and the meaning of a surface skin, whilst the expressive qualities of a decorative backdrop are often utilized within film mise-en-scènes. The design for the Coen Brothers' 1991 film *Barton Fink* utilizes a decorative skin of wallpaper to visually convey the infecting presence of a serial killer. The claustrophobic, cinematic, unhealthy, inner world of the run-down Hotel Earle literally emulates this character's emotional state: 'sweat drips off his forehead like the paper peels off the walls'[3] (Ciment and Niogret, 1991: 179). Production designer Dennis Gassner utilizes nauseously coloured green-and-yellow wallpaper to suggest 'an aura of putrefaction'[4] (ibid.: 179). This conscious mimicking of a film character's state of mind through the finished set highlights how a surface skin can visually enhance the psychological reading of interior

atmosphere. Both descriptions aim to illustrate this first response to the interior setting – through decisions relating to the surface treatment of space.

Layered skin

Layered skin can very simply be described as the placement of another surface next to, or on top of, the original setting. This layer is more substantial than the wallpaper or paint closely aligned to the first grouping as it typically includes the use of more robust textiles and materials, conceived to make them appear as a clear 'addition' to the original. This skin tends to 'echo' the original setting in its form, mimicking its shape and surface, enveloping and wrapping the interior. It can also subtly alter our perception through the use of layers that shield and camouflage. A layered skin can literally be placed over the original surface to instantly change the interior to its most current incarnation. The following descriptions aim to illustrate this second response to the interior setting, through decisions relating to layering.

At its simplest a layered skin can literally be a canvas and the internationally renowned artist Damien Hirst, in a recent retrospective at the Tate Modern, London used a series of 'living' canvases as an additional 'hung' layer on the walls of the gallery. These canvases tell the story of perpetual life and death, a recurring theme often found in his work and in his kaleidoscope canvas series. Chrysalises attached to the canvas surface saw 9,000 butterflies hatch, live and die. This cycle of life utilized the device of a layered skin rethought as a living, animate surface, an interesting twist on more conventional approaches to the

Figure 3.3
'I Am Become Death, Shatterer of the Worlds', 2006, Tate Modern retrospective, London, England, 2012 **by artist Damien Hirst.** Layered skin – a supersized canvas from Hirst's kaleidoscope series forms a layered skin imposed on the gallery walls that offers visual interest. Created through the use of gloss paint and butterfly wings, the pattern is reminiscent of ecclesiastical stained glass and relates to the artist's recurring themes of life and death.

decorative layer. In contrast to Hirst, the German artist Hans Hemmert plays with our perceptions by using air and latex to smother space. Titled 'Saturday Afternoon at Home in Neukölin', from 1995, the living room in his apartment in Berlin becomes concealed or cloaked behind a layer of bright-yellow latex forcing us to 'intuit the objects'[5] (Guidi, 1998: 01). This all-persuasive use of just one material serves to illustrate the psychological inner world of the artist through his artistic practice, but it also highlights how layered space can potentially distort our perception of interior space by quickly changing its nature.

Manipulated skin

Manipulated skin is primarily concerned with how the skin can be pulled, pinched or extruded. Through this process it takes on a life and character all of its own, typically giving a new personality to what was a fairly conventional flat setting. As a decorative layer it clings to the original surface whilst becoming self-consciously low relief; it has to 'set' like the icing on a cake. It needs to be formed of a material that is robust enough to hold this new shape, so plaster, metal and timber are employed to good effect here (although these materials are not exclusive to this category as it is how they are used that defines them). The following description aims to illustrate this third response to the interior setting through decisions relating to the manipulation of the skin of the space.

One of the most famous examples of an Aesthetic interior is the The Peacock Room, implemented by architect Thomas Jeckyll, but sensationally hijacked in 1877 by the artist James McNeill Whistler (1834–1903). It showcases a partially manipulated skin in the creation of a work of art that you could literally walk into. The room is designed as a suitable setting for the owner's collection of Chinese porcelain; the ceiling is manipulated into plaster light fixtures that erupt as stalactites from the flat surface, whilst the extruded wall surface seamlessly absorbs the bespoke shelving. The gold and Prussian blue colour scheme alongside Whistler's peacock paintings homogenize the interior, clearly illustrating how the manipulation of the decorative layer helped to create this elaborate period setting.

3.4

Figure 3.4
The Peacock Room, 1877, London (now housed at the Smithsonian Institute, Washington DC), by artist James McNeill Whistler and architect Thomas Jeckyll. Manipulated skin – in this historic example plaster is pulled and pinched until it erupts from the ceiling surface, whilst low-relief mouldings act as extrusions from the wall emphasized by the bespoke display system.

Three-dimensional skin

In contrast to the previous groupings, three-dimensional skin liberates itself from the confines of the original setting, suggesting a skin that spatially has aspirations to independence. This type of skin is often ambiguous, questioning its original decorative purpose as purely that of a setting. It is often used to create space or form furniture, alongside its original intent of defining the walls, floors or ceilings of a room. This skin, through its character and relationship to the original space, is visually distinctly separate but, most importantly, it has spatial and functional dimensions. The following description aims to illustrate this three-dimensional response to the skin of the interior setting.

Spatial dynamics remain central to American architect Denari's *oeuvre* as his work evidences a preoccupation with movement, aeronautical and spatial systems. His published books *Interrupted Projections* (1996) and *Gyroscopic Horizons* (1999) introduce respectively surface and terrain mapping. Bearing this theoretical stance in mind, Denari's design for l.a.Eyeworks' Los Angeles store, a leading designer optician, employs a

**Figure 3.5
l.a.Eyeworks, Los Angeles, USA, 2002 by Neil M. Denari Architects (NMDA).**
Three-dimensional skin –this type of skin is illustrated perfectly by Denari's trademark mapped forms. Rather than just adhering to the surfaces of the room, a three-dimensional skin is ambiguous in nature, aiming to blur the distinction between setting, space and furniture.

3.5

simple spatial strategy: 'the design shapes space and movement through a continuous suspended surface'[6] (Denari–NMDA, 2002). This linear folded strip begins its journey at the store entrance forming the canopy and signage. It then becomes absorbed into the dropped ceiling, furniture, display cabinets, bench and sales counter as it dynamically wends its way through the interior. These are typical attributes of a three-dimensional skin as it takes on a multitude of other functions, becoming more than just a visually appealing surface. It aims to transform your perception of the space by altering the existing spatial volume of the interior. These are all recurring virtues of a three-dimensional skin as it typically strives to embrace other properties by shunning its purely decorative role.

Examples of interior mise-en-scène, creating an interior setting

The examples that follow aim to give a more in-depth analysis of the design and use of an interior setting, and build on the introductory descriptions and attributes already detailed in the first half of this chapter. The choice of examples is once again deliberately diverse, ranging from the purely cinematic through to the historical, encompassing temporary, artistic and commercial incarnations of the interior. Their selection aims to illustrate how material and decorative decisions can have a significant impact on the atmospheric quality of an interior mise-en-scène.

Case Study One: Surface skin – *The Cabinet of Dr. Caligari*, director Robert Wiene

The sets of Caligari are painted … Everything has been subordinated to visual effect, to create a nightmare atmosphere, to arouse anxiety and terror.[7]

(Barsacq, [1970] 1976: 25)

Context

The iconic mise-en-scène for *The Cabinet of Dr. Caligari*, produced in 1919, remains influential to this day because of its interpretation of German expressionism, an artistic movement that was interested in the subjective. It aimed to express emotion rather than just render a faithful pictorial copy of the physical reality of the world. This conscious intertwining of the physical with the emotional was graphically realized through the surface skin of the set, and this is the reason why this case study has been included. As Herwarth Walden, founder of the Sturm Gallery stated:

Expressionism is neither a style nor a movement; it is a Weltanschauung [perception of the world].[8]

(Walden, cited in Robinson, [1997] 1999: 33)

Between the World Wars, Germany became closely associated with this form of expressionism at a time of great social, political and economic instability. It became an intensely creative and influential centre for artistic film-making that for a short period rivalled Hollywood. Directed by Robert Wiene, the film centres upon a mad doctor, the Caligari of the title, who controls a sleepwalking Cesare and uses him to perform a series of murders within the screenplay.

Approach to the physical setting, its skin

The film's setting utilized simple flat surfaces of stretched canvas painted with exaggerated light and shadow and is a clear example of surface skin. This setting deliberately set out to distort the interior and exterior spaces into painted abstract graphic scenes. Director Robert Wiene, designer Hermann Warm, and two painters, Walter Röhrig and Walter Reimann, collaborated on the design, deliberately exploring an expressionistic approach to the set that evoked a claustrophobic, nightmarish vision so that:

Every detail of every set is subjugated to the rigor [*sic*] of Expressionist distortion.[9]

(Sennett, 1994: 35)

This was partly a result of the production being filmed on a closed set rather than on location, where every aspect of the environment could be carefully controlled.

Narrative

The film is regarded as the most pervasive example of German expressionism by many; its expressionistic skin sought to cinematically contribute towards a narrative that communicated the psychosis of the villain. This setting was complemented by actors who wore stylized costumes and extraordinary make-up, whilst deliberately skewed and elongated props echoed the painted skin with its graphic distortions and abstract motifs. The acting for some of the main characters was deliberately mannered, using exaggerated movement and gestures.

All of the elements described above contributed towards an arresting atmosphere and an early cinematic example of surface skin. Its application illustrates how a carefully conceived interior setting contributed towards a mise-en-scène that concentrated upon engendering a sense of fear in its audience. This remains an interesting proposition for the design of interiors, and this becomes a significant moment culturally as the emotional became aligned to the introverted world of the interior.

3.6

Figure 3.6
The Cabinet of Dr. Caligari, **1919, director Robert Wiene.** Surface skin – expressionist painterly techniques, stark contrasts of painted light and dark combined with skewed forms and shapes are used to create a psychological setting that aims to illustrate through its scenography Caligari's domination and inner mental turmoil.

Case Study Two: Surface skin – Rough Luxe Hotel, Rabih Hage

The way I worked on the interiors was by taking off layers and putting very little back on. All revealed layers and added layers are authentic. We discovered wallpaper from 1936 under decades of paint. I peeled away strips of wallpaper that were stuck together until I reached a beautiful layer and stopped there.[10]

(Hage, cited in Lee, 2011: 308–9)

Context

The Rough Luxe Hotel helped to define a philosophy through an approach to the renovation of interiors that celebrated the past lives and incarnations of a building. Designed by architect Rabih Hage in 2008, it occupies a Grade II listed site, built in the 1800s in King's Cross, a run-down area of London that was undergoing major redevelopment at the time. The hotel as a brand aimed to rethink and redefine the term 'luxury', paralleling a shift in society away from the new and highly finished towards a more ethical one of upcycling and reuse.

Hage is credited with originating the term 'rough luxe', a stance that now defines a global philosophical approach to the interior concerned with preservation and 'the beauty of imperfection'[11] (ibid.: 308). This case study has been included because of its iconic re-imagining of the decorative surface as a narrative source.

3.7

Approach to the physical setting, its skin

The heritage site in King's Cross was instrumental in developing a response that respected the original setting through a process of revelation. This is a clear example of surface skin as Hage with surgical precision 'unpicked' the decades-old layers of wallpaper and paint to expose its earlier incarnations. This approach invites a tactile response as the strata of history can literally be felt beneath your fingertips. The history of the interior is laid bare: its past lives are revealed, immortalized and treasured for all to see and enjoy through this process of archaeological renovation. Hage even refers to himself as an 'urban archaeologist'[12] (cited in Niesewand, 2010: 93).

3.8

Figures 3.7, 3.8 and 3.9
Rough Luxe Hotel, London, England, 2008, by Rabih Hage.
Surface skin – in the interiors of this hotel an archaeological process of revelation exposes the surface skin; its layers of history are revealed through haptic and narrative concerns.

However, it was not all about a process of revelation; a new layer was added in the Breakfast Room developed around ideas of illusion. Working with architectural photographs of iconic Italian buildings, digital printed images were applied to the ceiling and walls of the room. These linings are photographs of actual places and their application at such a human scale aims to expand the small room spatially. This wallpaper becomes yet another story that hopes to transport you to a different time and place.

Narrative

The resultant interior mise-en-scène is concerned with the surface of the skin as a 'palimpsest', a layer upon which the new and old happily coexist. It is clear that Hage is interested in the 'authenticity' of the 'preserved' decorated skin as a narrative that has its own story to tell. The interior becomes the location upon which the aesthetic choices of the previous occupants are displayed, as Hage himself said:

'I'm like a time traveller, exposing the narrative of a building by revealing its past, and improving upon it'[13]

(ibid.: 93).

By primarily removing rather than just adding, an unusual position for a designer to take, this is a clear example of surface skin, which suggests that the patina and age of a building, if valued, can proffer an alternative approach to decoration and refurbishment that highlights storytelling.

3.9

Case Study Three: Manipulated skin – Strawberry Hill, Horace Walpole

But I do not mean to defend by argument a small capricious house. It was built to please my own taste, and in some degree to realize my own visions.[14]

(Walpole, [1784] 2015: 398)

Context

Horace Walpole (1717–97) is remembered not only for his bitingly caustic political journals and letters chronicling Georgian society, but also for the house he created in Twickenham, London. Bought as a summer residence, the house was originally a modest building on the banks of the River Thames. Walpole, a confirmed bachelor, son of the British Prime Minister Robert Walpole, famously wrote the first Gothic novel published in 1764 entitled *The Castle of Otranto*. These were tales written to send a shiver of delightful distaste through polite society. In keeping with this burgeoning sense of the Gothic, you would expect a best-selling Gothic author to live in a Gothic castle. Strawberry Hill became the epitome of Walpole's self-expression, allowing him to create the perfect fictional ancestral home. This became one of the most visited, documented and possibly one of the most well-known houses of the eighteenth century. This case study has been included because of its Gothic decorative excess and its exemplary manipulated skin.

Approach to the physical setting, its skin

The interior setting aims to create a fictional backdrop for Walpole as a teller of tales and as an obsessive connoisseur and dilettante who collected historical artefacts, paintings and objects. The sole purpose of the house with its extraordinary decorated skin was to serve as a suitable backdrop for the collection, revealing the stories of the pieces displayed. This is a classic example of a manipulated skin; the physical setting is a decorative exercise of illusion and artifice persuaded into low-relief forms that emulate the Gothic. In the Library, woodwork is coaxed into shape and painted to resemble the delicate filigree tracery of Gothic stonework, complemented by an elaborate painted ceiling suggesting low-relief ornamentation. *Trompe l'œil* wallpaper suggests plasterwork in the Entrance Hall; ancestral heraldic imagery abounds; whilst the famous plaster fan vaulting in the Gallery picked out in white and gold leaf is actually made of papier mâché. Walpole's exuberant decorative vision was pillaged from a wide range of medieval buildings, creating a hybrid interior that became, over time, his personal Gothic fantasy.

Narrative

This extraordinary interior mise-en-scène with its Gothic skin and pervading atmosphere became the 'go to' interior of its day. Walpole coined a term for this mood – 'gloomth'[15] (Snodin, 2009: 16), a combination of gloom and warmth, but this is not the dark Gothic we are familiar with. Instead, he was interested in creating a series of contrasting atmospheres, a form of 'mood journey'[16] (Snodin, n.d.) that consciously moved the visitor from gloom to light and colour, played with scale, and juxtaposed open vistas against interior introversion. Antique stained glass was used extensively to enhance the quality of light. Imagine this setting glinting in candlelight, the colours intensified by pools of concentrated shadow supported by its cast of artefacts. The joyful fakery of the skin is teased, pulled and pinched into a variety of forms, consciously manipulated to encourage a particular Gothic-revival effect. This historic Gothic carapace is justifiably important because its extensively documented decorative scheme was used to reinforce an individual's celebrity, an early example that reconciles the private decoration of a home with public persona. This is a role that interiors continue to aspire to and assume.

3.10

3.11

Figures 3.10 and 3.11 Strawberry Hill, London, England, created between 1748 and 1790 by Horace Walpole. Manipulated skin – 3.10 The Gothic carapace of Walpole's house is composed of papier mâché and plaster; in the Gallery this is coaxed into elaborate pinnacles, gilded ribs and white vaulting that reinforces his celebrity status. 3.11 *Trompe l'œil* wallpaper suggests plasterwork in the Entrance Hall and this decorative ambience is reinforced by the pervading sense of 'gloomth' – Walpole's highly personal interpretation of a Gothic atmosphere.

Case Study Four: Layered skin – 'Re-Set', Petra Blaisse

Textiles have emotions. They can have an enormous influence on the acoustics and the feel of the architecture. With one movement, you can create a totally different world, in every sense of the word – light, acoustics, color [*sic*], atmosphere, organization of space.[17]

(Blaisse, cited in Rajagopal 2013)

Context

Petra Blaisse is a Dutch interior and landscape designer who is best known for her textile interventions with her practice 'Inside Outside'. Her work plays with, and questions, the thresholds and boundaries that mark the divide, as well as the relationship, between interior and exterior space. Her material dressings (often in the form of curtains) are more than just decorative additions; they are intelligent in their response to specific environments. They typically shape the interior climate through the control of light and sound, developing a dialogue with the site, as well as in some cases forming space itself. It is this sensitive site dialogue mediated by the introduction of a new textile layer that justifies this case study's inclusion.

The 'Re-Set' project located within the Dutch pavilion (originally designed by Gerrit Rietveld in 1954) was conceived as a temporary remodelling of the interior for the 13th International Architecture Exhibition, Venice Biennale, 2012.

Approach to the physical setting, its skin

Blaisse's response to the pavilion is a beautiful example of a layered skin that matches the scale of the interior that houses it architecturally.

Full-height curtains were installed in the building, their presence reconfiguring the interior of the pavilion by introducing a skin of soft fabric that acts as a new mobile layer. This layer was mechanized via a simple track attached to the ceiling that allowed the curtains to glide slowly through the interior. This performance, a form of architectural choreography, was augmented by mechanical sounds introduced to enhance the sensory experience as the curtains slowly circulated. This textile reanimation drew inspiration from, but remained critical of, a building that remained unused during the majority of the year, only springing to life for events such as these.

Narrative

The host building was reconfigured by three curtains that introduced new material layers into the interior setting. These moving curtains, through their differing transparencies, opacities, colour, finish and spatial configurations, created a continually shifting sensory panorama, an ongoing narrative. Different aspects of the pavilion and its surroundings were first concealed and then revealed by these textural coverings. Mirrors mounted on the roof of the building reflected ever-changing natural light into the pavilion, whilst the movement of the curtains with their shimmering, ever-changing qualities of light and shade altered continually. This was augmented by the whisper of the mechanism and the rustle of the curtains, a direct result of the addition of this material layer. This is a clear example of a layered skin, but a layered skin that seeks to develop an animated architectural narrative of change rather than constancy. For Blaisse, the curtains perform, entering into a dialogue with the building by creating a series of sensory encounters and experiences for the user. It is these transformative qualities and the resultant ever-changing interior mise-en-scène that reconsider and highlight for any design student the decorated interior as a venue of sensory performance and spectacle.

3.12

Figures 3.12, 3.13 and 3.14 **'Re-Set', Venice, Italy, 2012, by Petra Blaisse (Inside Outside).** Layered skin – Blaisse introduces her trademark soft skin of material, layering it into the existing building. This mechanized textile covering offers an ever-changing sensory performance of light, shade, reflection and shifting panoramas introducing kinetic concerns to the design of the interior.

Case Study Five: Three-dimensional skin – KU64 Kids Club, GRAFT

We like to tell a good story, and we like it if everyone can relate to it.[18]

(GRAFT in Blomberg, Waldsee and GRAFT, 2011: 15)

Context

GRAFT, an architectural practice founded in Germany but now with offices internationally, are interested in telling stories, viewing this as the common currency that strives to connect the user to the space they inhabit. For them,

'stories can be understood and experienced by everyone, as they are easy to access'[19]

(ibid.: 95).

The name GRAFT, chosen by the practice's founding members, relates to hybridization or the fusion of one or more systems, and this is what they set out to achieve within their designed environments. They are interested in creating spatially ambiguous landscapes that have enough 'interestingness'[20] (ibid.: 15) to engage the curious user through the introduction of multiple meanings.

KU64, completed in 2011, is a children's dentist situated on the top floor of an office building in Berlin, Germany. It has been included as a useful example of a three-dimensional skin that is central to the interior's new narrative.

Approach to the physical setting, its skin

Starting from the premise that, for many, a visit to the dentist has negative overtones, the fears of the patient are often heightened by the sound of the dental drill and the clinical environment. GRAFT set out to 'alter' this reality through the conceptual introduction of a 'trip to the beach'[21] (ibid.: 102). This is a clear example of a three-dimensional skin that becomes liberated from its confines, freed to form a series of undulations and contours that suggest sand dunes. These sand dunes create independent spaces of play and adventure, even inverting to hang from the ceiling. This three-dimensional landscape is further enhanced by the inclusion of a secret garden, in reality a vertical green wall, whilst the waiting room extends the story by offering a notional campfire set amongst the dunes.

The pervasive use of the colour yellow via a polyurethane surface reinforces the concept of the sand dune visually. Additional graphic images of a person jumping are printed onto its surface at key points within the interior. These printed images employ a technique known as 'anamorphic distortion' whereby the viewer has to stand in a particular position to view the image. This becomes another layer of 'interestingness' for GRAFT.

3.15

Narrative

The interior mise-en-scène of KU64 sets out to psychologically 'distract' from the perceived reality of a trip to the dentist. The transformation of the original perimeter skin of the space into an ambiguous three-dimensional landscape of canted walls, floors and sloping ceilings even absorbs the furniture into this new spatial topography. The space is reinvented and re-imagined by its skin into new configurations; its setting is transformed. In this dentist's surgery nothing is as you would expect. The inclusion of multiple readings within the interior helps to create stories to engage and distract the young patient, and it is this process of psychological distraction that resonates within the context of this book. For its young audience, the interior becomes transformed as a space where the imagination can roam, whilst the three-dimensional skin suggests how space can be created once a decorative layer is rethought as something inherently spatial.

Figures 3.15, 3.16 and 3.17 KU64 Kids Club, Berlin, Germany, 2011, by GRAFT. Three-dimensional skin – the interior of this dentist's surgery illustrates a skin that liberates itself from the confines of the original setting to create spaces, walls and furniture. This ambiguous re-imagining of the decorative surface literally tells a story.

3.16

3.17

Conclusion

This chapter aimed to introduce, and increase, your understanding of the interior setting through a greater awareness of the decorative skin in line with the chapter focus. The four categories of surface, layered, manipulated, and three-dimensional skin were introduced merely as devices to help facilitate debate concerning the diverse properties of this covering. Of especial interest was the role the interior setting could take atmospherically, and whether this reinforced the idea of an interior mise-en-scène.

The Cabinet of Dr. Caligari and Walpole's Strawberry Hill both use their interior setting expressively, and this is aligned with the demonstrative qualities of mise-en-scène. The former is important within the study of interiors as it highlights cinematically how the design of the interior setting became imbued with emotion. The film's celebrated mise-en-scène attempted to capture and communicate to its audience the troubled psychological mental state of its main character. The set became conceived as something inherently nightmarish, an approach that undoubtedly corresponded to the collective psyche of a world recently at war, alongside all the attendant horrors that this unleashed. It is surely no coincidence that this was also the juncture that saw the rise of German expressionism and the birth of psychiatry. Through this troubled view of the world came the desire to create something that resonated with this newly formed reality, so the interior became a place of torment as well as beauty. Clearly, any examination of interior atmosphere needs to consider the good, the bad and the ugly if it is to be fully comprehended.

In a similar manner Walpole, as the celebrated Georgian Gothic author, is an early example of how the design of a private home also served as a public space that reinforced an individual's persona and celebrity. Strawberry Hill's extensive use of 'gloomth' as an atmospheric mood journey, supported by its extensive collection of artefacts, was undoubtedly reinforced by its elaborate interior setting and Gothic backdrop. This approach corresponds to a trait Walter Benjamin identified through his writings, an attribute (which was introduced in Chapter One) of the home as the locus of self-expression and display. The physical skin of this interior is clearly aligned with this intent, suggesting decoration can reinforce identity (corresponding to how production design can be used to communicate a character's traits).

Both Hage and GRAFT use the decorative setting as a revelatory skin that links to storytelling. Hage, through his veneration of history and authenticity, reclaims, reuses and exposes materials. The interior setting of the Rough Luxe Hotel acts as a narrative backdrop – a revelatory skin – that through a process of deconstruction discloses its own history through its tactile decorative layers. This stratum of history, rather than being hidden, is celebrated, creating a bespoke interior narrative. In a similar manner GRAFT's re-imagining of a trip to the dentist becomes aligned with a fictitious adventure. The conventional dentist's surgery interior is abandoned. Instead, they aim to distract patients through storytelling from the real reason for their visit. The undulating yellow skin highlights how the interior setting can be given meaning by reinforcing an imported narrative.

Finally, Blaisse's textile coverings serve to animate the interior through a sensory choreography, a decision that transformed the interior into a kinetic experience that reportedly captivated its audience. This newly installed layering of soft skin serves to illustrate how this simple decorative device, perceptually and acoustically, can transform interior space.

This approach, whilst highlighting the sensory qualities of the interior, brings performance into the realm of interior design, and clearly this is a central concern of any mise-en-scène. The intention of these concluding chapter case studies is that they should all clearly illustrate the role that the interior setting, through its decorative skin, has in informing atmosphere both aesthetically and psychologically, as well as reinforcing its role as a central ingredient of a mise-en-scène for the interior.

FURTHER READING – EXPLORING THE INTERIOR SETTING

This chapter has concentrated upon the interior setting as a scenic backdrop that through its choice and use of materiality has expressive, narrative qualities. Opportunities for the continued exploration of this idea are included through some further readings. Central to this stance is the notion that decoration can become more than just surface ornamentation, as given the right opportunity it can experientially alter our perception of a given space.

'The Five Senses: Boxes' (2011) by French philosopher Michel Serres succinctly outlines his concept of the interior of the house as an 'orthopaedic sensorium' that encloses the body. Here, the interior setting becomes a series of layered tactile skins. This abridged essay is located in Lois Weinthal's comprehensive compendium of interior theory titled *Towards a New Interior: An Anthology of Interior Design Theory*, whilst the full text can be found in Serres' book, *The Five Senses, a Philosophy of Mingled Bodies* (2008).

Rough Luxe Design: The New Love of the Old (2011) by Kahi Lee brings together in one volume many of the leading exponents of the Rough Luxe movement. In a shared love of the old, a surface patina of age becomes integral to the story and previous life of the materials used. This philosophy helped to re-evaluate interior decoration by questioning its endless quest for the new, and replacing this with a reverence for aged authenticity.

Kurt Schwitters' Merzbau: The Cathedral of Erotic Misery (2000) by Elizabeth Burns Gamard represents an exhaustively researched and comprehensive study of artist Schwitters' 'Merzbau'. His labyrinthine architectural installation reconsidered its plaster skin of re-purposed found objects as a surface concerned with personal expression, acting as a mimetic device that reflected Schwitters' many obsessions and preoccupations.

4

What is an interior 'prop'?

Accessories, furniture, fixtures and equipment

One need only study with due exactitude the physiognomy of the homes of great collectors. Then one would have the key to the nineteenth century interior. Just as in the former case the objects gradually take possession of the residence, so in the latter it is a piece of furniture that would retrieve and assemble the stylistic traces of the centuries.[1]

(Benjamin, [1982] 2002: 218)

4.1

Figure 4.1
'Props', sets and props waiting to be loaded for a journey to York, 1947.
This chapter will explore the role of interior 'props', specifically how accessories, furniture, fixtures and equipment can enhance and give meaning to the interior setting.

Introducing interior props

Props within film and the theatre are generally regarded as movable items that the main characters come into contact with, in other words, objects that are used on stage that are distinct from the scenery or setting. They help to underline and communicate the personality of the characters, as well as giving visual 'clues' that relate to the film's narrative. They also contribute towards the creation of a specific atmosphere or locale.

Within an interior the definition of a prop is by nature fairly wide-ranging, its scale changing to work within the setting it finds itself. It could be an accessory such as an *objet d'art* that embellishes the look of the interior, or it could relate to the choice of loose furniture that enhances the ambience. It can become a fixture, something that is more permanently fitted to the interior setting, through to the choice of equipment that characterizes it. The scale ranges to encompass something you could literally hold in your hand, to a prop as a free-standing object that becomes a habitable space. The following points underline the focus of this chapter.

CHAPTER FOCUS

- An introduction to the role of 'props' within interior design.
- An exploration of design approaches that utilize interior props through the four categories of accessories, furniture, fixtures, and equipment.
- An investigation of interior props and their role in the creation of an interior mise-en-scène.

Using interior props

For any designer who is concerned with the creation, design and assemblage of the physical environment of an interior, both the setting and the props work together to communicate a certain ambience, define space, and suggest its habitation. Additionally, they bring a richness of tactile and textural detail that invites the touch. These props can be loosely identified through four categories, which are:

1. Accessories;
2. Furniture;
3. Fixtures;
4. Equipment.

Each of these categories will be discussed in more detail through the following descriptions and in the more detailed case studies to follow. The term 'furniture, fixtures and equipment' (or 'FF&E' for short) is prevalent within the design industry and relates to items that have no permanent connection to the structure of the building or its utilities. Many design companies offer an FF&E service as part of a design package.

Accessories

Accessories can be defined as anything that 'embellishes' the interior such as ornaments, art, sculptures, lighting (if loose), mirrors, even soft furnishings such as cushions and curtains, which represents a typical, but not exhaustive, list. They are used within the interior to give a sense of habitation, of a 'lived in' space informed by the possessions it contains. They can pique your interest as a visitor, often saying something about the person, company or brand they belong to – after all, taste is very subjective, often linked to class and cultural connotations. These possessions can also be invested with psychological meaning, acquiring emotional significance way beyond their monetary value. Designers can play with these rules and often do by 'dressing' a space to gain a particular effect. The following descriptions aim to illustrate this first category of props relating to the use of accessories chosen for their theatricality, as much as for their deliberate artifice.

The Hollywood designer Tony Duquette (1914–99), protégé of society decorator Elsie de Wolfe, famously used accessories in the creation of exuberant interior set pieces. Completed in 1949, Dawnridge, the designer's Los Angeles home, showcased Duquette's signature theatrical style. The maximalist interiors wear an elaborate costume of silks and faux jewels whereby every conceivable surface is overflowing with personal ornaments and curios. This example clearly highlights how accessories can both personalize and bring a strong visual identity to interior space by reflecting the personality of the owner to the outside world. Accessories or small props in

Figure 4.2
Dawnridge, Los Angeles, USA, 1949, by designer Tony Duquette.
Props as accessories – accessories are central to the creation of a decorated interior and this styled space aims to convey a particular look whilst simultaneously communicating the personality of the owner.

film work along similar lines as the Duquette interior, and this is clearly seen in *A Woman in Black* based upon the novel by Susan Hill. Rather than reflecting the personality of the owner, these props instead reinforce the character of the film as a period ghost story. Starring Daniel Radcliffe as the recently widowed Arthur Kipps, the action is centred upon the isolated Eel Marsh House, brought to life by production designer Kave Quinn. The film builds a suitably dark atmosphere through shadows and candlelight, decaying decorated rooms, peopled by a cast of authentic Victorian automatons and artefacts. These Gothic props include 'taxidermy figures, bizarre children's toys, creepy porcelain dolls and eerie family portraits with the eyes scratched out'[2] (Groskop, 2012). They all aim to heighten the disturbing ambience of the film, illustrating how props can contribute towards atmospheric perception.

Furniture

Furniture can be defined as 'loose' items that can be easily removed, such as desks, chairs, bookcases, tables and office partitions. The use of the term in this instance relates to free-standing, movable items that have no permanent connection to the building. As props, furniture can suggest a certain usage; it helps to define spatial territories by suggesting zones and rooms for activities; it also creates space for social encounters. Furniture can be formal or relaxed depending upon the circumstances it finds itself in, whilst its choice aesthetically, alongside its arrangement, can influence how we perceive the finished interior. The following descriptions illustrate this second category of props by highlighting how they can be used to create habitable interior landscapes that inform atmosphere.

Interior architects i29 define their approach as one that concentrates upon the spatial; they have used furniture as props in a series of office schemes to help define space. Their interior scheme for Combiwerk Delft, a company that aims to reintegrate into the workplace people with learning difficulties or physical limitations, is typical of this approach. Whilst the building was designed by VMX Architects, i29 concentrated on populating the interior by utilizing both bespoke and existing furniture grouped into coloured clusters (red, green, yellow, and blue), alongside carpets that

Figures 4.3 and 4.4
Combiwerk Delft, Netherlands, 2012, by i29 Interior Architects.
Props as furniture – loose furniture is grouped to create coloured zones of occupation demarcating spatial territory by suggesting 'hubs' of habitable space for its user.

took on the same tone. Territories of habitation are suggested by this colour coding, whilst continuity through the reuse of existing and secondhand chairs was integrated into the scheme for a user that is psychologically averse to change. Furniture can also be central to filmed space and, cinematically, *Playtime*, released in 1967, directed by and starring Jacques Tati (1907–82), highlights the use of furniture spatially through an enormous modernist set. 'Tativille' (as the set became known) was developed by Tati's collaborator, production designer Jacques Lagrange. Tati, as the increasingly baffled character of Monsieur Hulot, attempts to navigate his way through this uncompromising urban environment. The office remains one of the most memorable scenes, with its seemingly endless array of impersonal office cubicles, free-standing props that defined space by creating a room for just one worker. In a similar manner to the previous example, this cinematic interior illustrates how furniture can demarcate individual rooms within a larger area, characterize space, as well as inform social encounters. Here, it is taken to the extreme in its critique of modernism.

Figure 4.5
'NY-11-18-02-10', New York, USA, 2010, by Campaign.
Props as fixtures – fixtures can have a spatial dimension; here, they are used temporarily to divide and demarcate space whilst reinforcing a fashion brand narrative.

Fixtures

Fixtures, in contrast to the loose furniture discussed above, form a distinct category as they are 'fitted' or attached to the building framework, are reasonably permanent but can be removed if necessary. They have no impact upon the building's structure, are often bespoke pieces designed and constructed to fit a specific location, although they can equally be readily available bought systems – typically, partitions, bookshelves, fitted kitchens or fitted furniture. It is worth noting that lighting becomes a fixture if it can no longer be unplugged or moved. Fixtures are sometimes referred to as fittings; the two words are interchangeable but the definition remains the same. The following descriptions aim to illustrate this third category of props relating to the use of fixtures.

A temporary installation by Campaign during New York Fashion Week for fashion brand Dunhill illustrates fixtures as a category. Located in a disused warehouse in the Meatpacking District of New York, the design recreates founder Alfred Dunhill's Georgian home in London as an architectural apparition. In reality, this ghostly image is composed of aluminium panels cut to express the elevations of his residence. These fixtures are temporarily attached, suspended from the ceiling of the existing space to form a new room, and it is this spatial use of a fixture that makes it important. In contrast, The Hempel, a luxury hotel located in Knightsbridge, London (since converted into luxury apartments), was designed as a series of striking, minimal sets by actress-turned-designer Anouska Hempel. The serene lobby reduced the reception desk to a bespoke, monolithic slab of limestone that

4.6

Figure 4.6
The Hempel, London, England, 1997, by Anouska Hempel Design. Props as fixtures – fixed bespoke fixtures such as hotel reception desks are a typical example of this type of prop. As a key front-of-house space, the hotel lobby aims to communicate a specific message to prospective guests through its styling and scale.

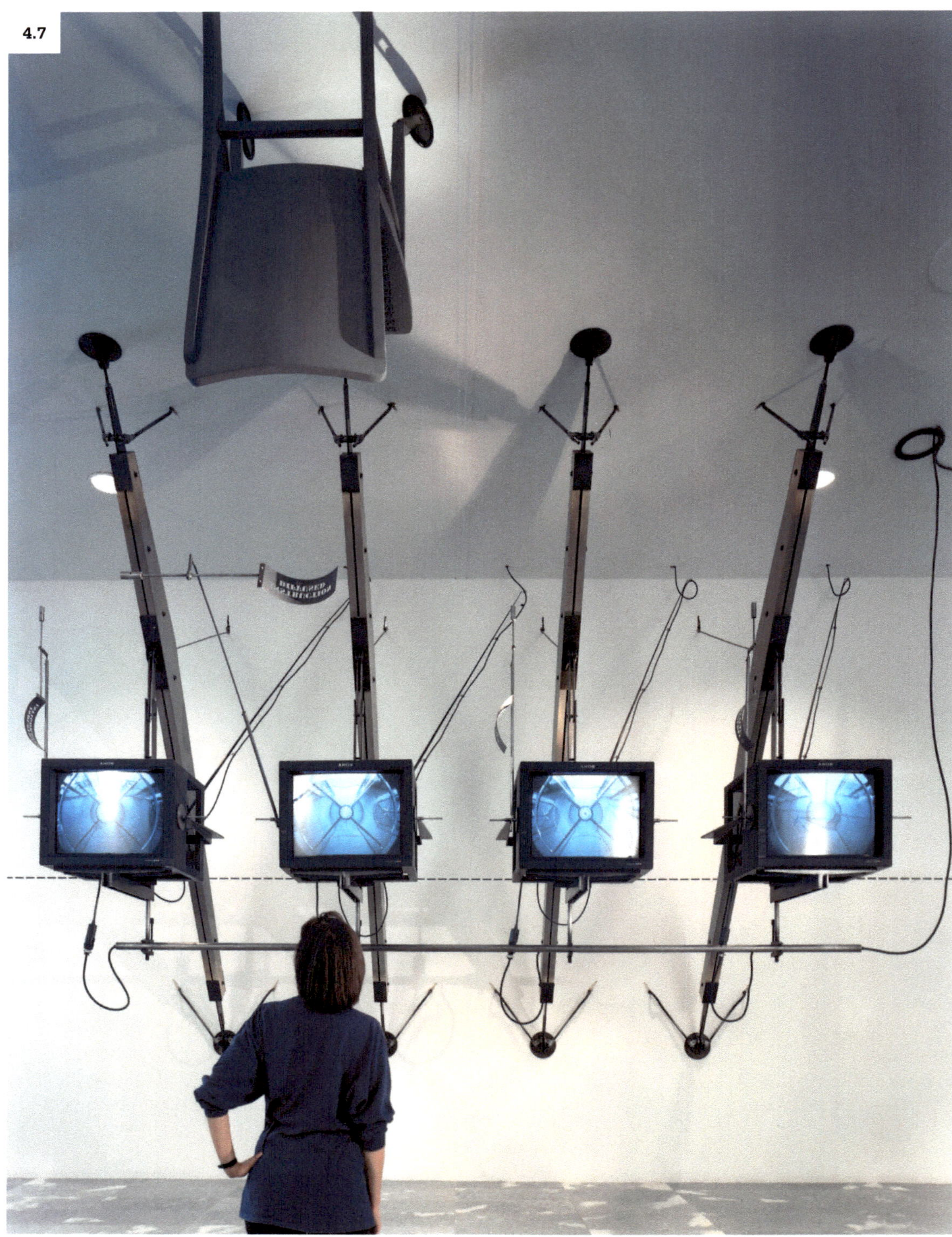

**Figure 4.7
'Para-site',
Museum of
Modern Art,
New York, USA,
by Diller +
Scofidio, 1989.**
Props as
equipment
– concerns
relating to display,
surveillance and
voyeurism are
reinforced by the
use of television
monitors, and this
choice of
equipment clearly
characterizes
interior space.

became a fixture within the interior, overseen by black-clad attendants. The pervading association of minimalism with luxury sent out a clear message regarding the high-end quality of this hotel to its prospective guests. This example highlights how specially designed fixtures can become a hierarchical element, whilst simultaneously investing that space with a particular ambience and meaning.

Equipment

Equipment as a grouping encompasses the electronic equipment and technologies we all encounter as we go about our lives, items that enable us to complete tasks at work or at home. It typically includes the more cumbersome, rather than the portable items we are familiar with today; white goods, large-screen computers or other specialist machinery all form part of this category. These items not only have a functional use but also an aesthetic one as they can characterize the interior, imbuing it with a certain personality. Designers are increasingly using equipment, whether this is the actual object or just its effect in order to enhance interiors; the following description aims to illustrate this final category of props through an example relating to the use of equipment.

The early work of Diller + Scofidio (now Diller, Scofidio + Renfro) highlights their recurring interest in display, surveillance and voyeurism. Their 'Para-site' installation, temporarily housed in the Museum of Modern Art in New York, utilized equipment to memorable effect. Cameras positioned at the museum's main entrances captured visitors on film as they arrived, which was then replayed through television monitors in the main galleries. These monitors were suspended within a parasitic structure complete with chair for the fictional viewer. As an assemblage of equipment, fixtures and furniture, their

installation highlights the impact that these elements, when combined, can have on the interior.

Examples of interior mise-en-scène, props and atmosphere

Included next is a selection of examples of mise-en-scène that explore further the use of interior props. Ranging through the four categories already discussed, it aims to highlight and illustrate how the physicality of the interior setting can be further enhanced by the props it contains. Following this train of thought to its logical conclusion, the setting becomes the literal backdrop or scenery of the space, whilst the accessories, furniture, fixtures and equipment are its props. For expediency, these examples will be analysed using the usual headings of context and narrative, whilst special attention will be focused on the 'use of props' by the introduction of this as an analytical category.

Case Study One: Accessories, furniture and fixtures – the Ace Hotel, Roman and Williams

We think more about the narrative, more about the experience, and the spaces sort of accumulate out of that.[3]

(Standefer, cited in Swanson, 2010)

Context

The Ace Hotel renovation by New York-based designers Roman and Williams is centrally located in mid-town just off Broadway. The building was originally built in 1904 as the Hotel Breslin and its inherent character was central to the subsequent renovation. Both Robin Standefer and Stephen Alesch of Roman and Williams have a background in film; this experience has helped them to develop an ethos that is less about style and more concerned with narrative. It is this interest in narrative that has led to their inclusion here, as their design for the Ace Hotel develops a storyline through the selection of accessories, furniture and fixtures.

Use of props

This approach is exemplified by the lobby of the Ace Hotel. The existing space, although in desperate need of some tender, loving care, had a strong turn-of-the-century architectural presence. This character was retained and formed the basis of the interior setting. By taking a curatorial role, and with an eye for detail, the designers sourced props for the interior, finding and selecting vintage pieces.

4.8

Accessories are liberally sprinkled throughout the interior – the ubiquitous taxidermy is displayed in cases and cabinets, whilst antique glass bottles line the tops of the cabinets. Salvaged over-scaled letters are prominently displayed, vintage lighting fixtures abound, whilst an American flag takes pride of place over the lobby bar. Even the books in the library have been carefully chosen. Furniture ranges from huge slate-topped laboratory tables, tartan wing-backed chairs, ex-school chairs and salvaged apothecary cabinets to a pair of massive red sofas designed in-house by the practice. The lobby bar is a literal room: a panelled library reclaimed as a complete fixture from a Park Avenue apartment and inserted whole into the space as a habitable prop.

Narrative

These former set and production designers fill the physical set with props and accessories; detail matters, aiming to develop a pervasive cinematic atmosphere realized as a fully formed, immersive fictional world. They use their props evocatively to reinforce the narrative and conjure up a particular time and place. Their first site visit to what would become the Ace Hotel revealed a building rich in history and architectural features, but with an air of decay and abandonment. It was this 'fugitive quality'[4] (Alesch and Standefer, 2012: 12) that inspired them as they imagined a narrative based upon:

a grand, dilapidated country house that The Doors holed up in to make a record, or maybe an old-money retreat where a kid threw a big party when his parents weren't around, and he and his friends trashed the place.[5]

(ibid.: 12)

Every prop is carefully selected to help stage this storyline, whilst the Ace Hotel lobby gives off the aura of an archetypal grand, if faded, European hotel. Its mise-en-scène captures a unique sense of time and place assembled through the dispersal of accessories, furniture and fixtures in a clear example of design through curation.

4.9

Figures 4.8 and 4.9
The Ace Hotel, New York, USA, 2009, by Roman and Williams. Props as accessories – the carefully curated accessories, furniture and fixtures in this hotel lobby help to evoke the atmosphere of a 'grand, dilapidated country house'. These former designers of film environments use props evocatively to reinforce this fictional narrative.

Case Study Two: Furniture – *A Clockwork Orange*, director Stanley Kubrick

This alienating décor is full of works of art. Fiber-glass nudes [*sic*], crouched like Playboy femlins in the Korova Milk Bar, serve as tables or dispense mescaline-laced milk from their nipples.[6]

(Hughes, 1971: 131–2)

Context

Released in 1971 and based upon the 1960s' novel by Anthony Burgess, *A Clockwork Orange* remains an influential film to this day. Directed by Stanley Kubrick (1928–99), the dystopian story, set in the not-too-distant future, explores the rise of a violent youth culture. Burgess famously created a whole new language for the story, known as 'nadsat', and the main character, Alex, and his 'droogs' (friends, associates) infamously commit random acts of 'ultra-violence'[7](Burgess [1962] 1982: 58).

Kubrick was undoubtedly central to the film's startling and controversial visual imagery. Whilst most of the film was shot on location, the few film sets developed by production designer John Barry have had a lasting impact, and it is this legacy that has led to this case study's inclusion. Interior props (in this instance, furniture) are successfully employed in the creation of an unsettling interior atmosphere.

Use of props

The opening sequence of *A Clockwork Orange*, set in the Korova Milk Bar, is undeniably important as it helps to set the tone of the film through the design of an interior that is psychologically uncomfortable. Memorably, the environment is formed by furniture, in this case 'furniture-mannequins', human figures based on the sexually submissive, if erotic, figures of woman. White fibreglass nudes, frozen into positions of abandonment, litter the interior of the milk bar; the only colour comes from their brightly coloured wigs and pubic hair, visible through their deliberately splayed legs. Other nudes, kneeling on plinths, dispense Korova cocktails – milk laced with your drug of choice from their bare nipples. The nudes were, in fact, inspired by the work of pop artist Allen Jones.

Narrative

The black interior pays homage to the sixties' 'pop art' that was prevalent at the time, but it is the use of props that elevates this scene. In a deliberate act of provocation for the viewing audience, these were props developed as fetish furniture that became the tables that Alex, his droogs and other punters rest both their feet and drinks upon. This is a carefully constructed interior tableau that, by positioning Alex at the centre of a fixed scene, resplendent in his all-white uniform, complete with codpiece and one false eyelash, manages to communicate an air of total control and menace reinforced by the use of music. It also implied an attitude to women that is borne out by the film to come. Perhaps unsurprisingly, the burgeoning feminist movement at the time criticized the film for both its portrayal of women and for glamorizing sexual violence. Beverley Walker's comments are often quoted to underline this point:

ugly, lewd and brutal toward the female human being: all of the women are portrayed as caricatures; the violence committed upon them is treated comically; the most startling aspect of the décor relates to the female form.[8]

(Walker, cited in Webster, 2011: 75)

With its deliberately eroticized furniture upon which is played out a violent battle of not just the sexes, but of society's values, this film reflected many of the themes that came to be associated with the sixties and seventies. Kubrick created a memorable, if confrontational, interior mise-en-scène. This example clearly illustrates how furniture can be used in the creation of an interior that is deliberately confrontational and psychologically disconcerting.

Figure 4.10
A Clockwork Orange, 1971, **director Stanley Kubrick.**
Props as furniture – the furniture within this film was designed to challenge its audience and psychologically taint the interior atmosphere. The actors, their costumes and stance, and the musical score all reinforce this unsettling mise-en-scène.

Case Study Three: Equipment – Break Down, Michael Landy

At the end of it all, I'll be left with nothing. For a moment perhaps escaping consumerism, but also at the same moment being the perfect person to sell it to.[9]

(Landy, 2001: 108)

Context

Michael Landy is a British artist, who through his work has explored and questioned 'contemporary consumerism'. Commissioned and financed by the Artangel Foundation in 2001, Break Down allowed him to examine consumerism from the point of view of himself as a consumer, by seeking an answer to the question:

'what is it that makes consumerism the strongest ideology of our time?'[10]

(ibid.: 114).

His temporary installation occupied an empty retail unit for two weeks in one of London's busiest retail districts – Oxford Street. It is the pervasive use of a specific interior prop, in this case, equipment, and its link to interior spectacle that has led to this case study's inclusion.

Use of props

This interior was defined by a 100-metre conveyor belt that formed four work bays and a sorting platform. The whole project was in preparation for three years, and Landy spent a substantial part of that time producing an inventory of all of his possessions. This list encompassed 7,227 belongings that included consumed or bought objects such as his car, a Saab Turbo, as well as cherished inherited personal possessions, typically, the sheepskin coat that originally belonged to his father.

Envisaged as one huge piece of equipment, Break Down was conceived as a temporary event, a performative piece that attracted huge crowds. The bright-blue conveyor belt, commissioned from a material reclamation company, was in a state of perpetual motion, displaying yellow containers filled with Landy's possessions. Blue-overall-clad operatives, with Landy as the site foreman, completed this busy scene. The stripped-out interior had that forlorn, uncared-for ambience common to many empty retail units, enlivened only by signs saying 'everything must go'. As the conveyor belt circulated, it revealed trays of objects in various stages of demolition; everything was catalogued and sorted according to its material, before being smashed and ground to a fine powder. At the end of this two-week period, Landy's former possessions had been reduced to nearly six tonnes of granulated rubbish, none of which was recycled; instead, it went to a landfill site – a decision calculated to underline the point of the whole exercise.

Narrative

This was, 'writ large', the story of Landy's life as a consumer and a parody of a traditional production line – rather than producing or manufacturing something, this one destructs. His installation brought into question our engendered shopping habits of continual consumption, or shopping as a form of therapy, and questioned both the social and sustainable cost. This could be viewed as a cathartic process, although destroying all of your possessions, even voluntarily, must have an emotional impact.

Here, equipment takes centre stage both visually and functionally, whilst the auditory ambience underlines the narrative of consumerism through a process of noisy destruction. The 'action' itself became the star, supported by a host of overall-clad actors in supporting roles. It is a theatre of industry, one full of noise and movement that celebrates the process of destruction; the specially commissioned machinery plays its role to perfection. Of special interest here is the impact that 'usage' as a core ingredient of atmosphere can have – a spatial consequence that is often overlooked and undervalued. Inhabited space through industrious activity can undoubtedly bring an interior to life and, in this instance, equipment is central to this populated interior mise-en-scène.

Figures 4.11 and 4.12 **Break Down, London, England, 2001, by artist Michael Landy.** Props as equipment – a specially commissioned conveyor belt characterizes the interior, offering spectacle through a manufactured performance of noise and destruction. Peopled by a host of operatives, this tells the artist's story.

4.11

4.12

Case Study Four: Fixtures – Maggie's Cancer Caring Centre, Frank Gehry

the atmosphere disarms the immediate mood. It displaces depression for the moment and allows one a place of reflection, of humour. It gives one perspective on a shared journey ahead, made with others in the same boat. Some doctors have spoken up very positively about these aspects of the centres.[11]

(Jencks, in Jencks and Heathcote, 2010: 42)

Context

Maggie's Cancer Caring Centres aim to provide support to anyone affected by cancer; central to this idea is the development of a culture within their buildings that offers a series of emotional, psychological and practical responses to living with cancer by nurturing an atmosphere of positivity. The developed interior atmosphere echoes this directive, leading to this case study's inclusion. Located within close proximity to a hospital, there are now a series of Maggie's Centres across Britain.

The first Maggie's Centre was inspired by the experiences of Maggie Keswick, wife of the architectural writer Charles Jencks, and has become her legacy. American architect Frank Gehry (who joins an illustrious rostrum of previously invited star-architects) was invited by Jencks to design the Dundee Centre, at Ninewells Hospital, Scotland, and it was completed in 2003. This was to be the first 'stand alone' building as the previous Maggie's Centres had all been conversions of existing buildings.

4.13

Use of props

Gehry describes his approach to the Dundee Centre through the use of a Yiddish term, '*Heymish*'[12] (Jencks and Heathcote, 2010: 114), meaning comfortable, friendly and homelike. A tower and a pleated roof create a series of interior spaces that respond to the needs of a Maggie's Centre. The kitchen is at the heart of the space, kitted out by a series of built-in fixtures: typically, fitted furniture that matches the scale of the building. Fixtures take centre stage as a huge, padded window seat occupies one side of the kitchen, whilst a run of fitted kitchen units occupies the other. Built-in shelving is filled with an array of books and toys, offering many opportunities for conversation or activity. These fixtures set the scene for a series of impromptu encounters that have the familiar sound and look of a domestic backdrop.

Narrative

Maggie's Centres take a particular approach to the design of their spaces. This arose out of what is unfortunately, for many, the reality of a hospital visit, encountering an alienating, functional and sterile interior that, for Maggie, became a form of 'architectural aversion therapy'[13] (Jencks, 2010: 12). Instead, the centres are designed with a deliberate air of informality known as 'kitchenism'[14] (ibid.: 34), a conceptual approach that celebrates the domestic and the small-scale. Props masquerading as kitchen fixtures dominate as places of informal everyday encounters, hoping to encourage a sense of normality.

For Jencks, these centres can make a difference to cancer patients by taking a holistic approach to the mind as well as the body, which he refers to as the 'architectural placebo effect'[15] (Rose, 2010). For him, the building takes a supporting role by simply amplifying the message of the carers and its community. Maggie's Centres have encouraged debate regarding how design can affect people's moods, developing ideas around a growing movement that considers 'wellness' through design. These centres with their air of informality and domestic ambience underline the value of considering the psychological impact that an interior environment can have on its end user.

Figures 4.13 and 4.14
Maggie's Cancer Caring Centre, Dundee, Scotland, 2003, by Frank Gehry.
Props as fixtures – the famous Maggie welcome is reinforced by an interior that emulates the domestic realm. Fixtures such as a fitted kitchen, tables and seating help to humanize the interior by suggesting informality and normality psychologically.

4.14

Case Study Five: Props as fixtures – Kesselskramer, FAT

Taste locates value on the surface of objects, that is, on their cultural reception rather than on their innate properties.[16]

(Charles Holland of FAT, in Jencks and FAT, 2011: 95)

Context

Kesselskramer's iconic office interior in Amsterdam, designed by FAT (an acronym for Fashion, Architecture, Taste) in 1998, successfully captured the zeitgeist by reconsidering the working environment as one of relaxed informality, surreal humour and storytelling. This case study has been included because it utilized interior props to overcome a restricted site, rethought your stereotypical office environment, whilst simultaneously ensuring that the right image for the company was projected to potential clients.

Kesselskramer are an international creative communications agency specializing in film and digital media, whilst FAT, renowned for work that actively questioned taste and meaning within design, were a multidisciplinary architectural studio (recently disbanded). Kesselskramer concentrate on getting brands to tell new stories and this approach has been applied to their re-imagined interior.

4.15

Use of props

This office was to be situated within a nineteenth-century Gothic church (originally linked to a Catholic order of nuns); the building carried heritage status so structural alterations were prohibited. This restriction inspired the renovation as carefully 'placed' bespoke objects became habitable props within the interior. These props populate a notional streetscape and visually came to life as everyday (if whimsical) objects: a lifeguard's watchtower, a fort and a shed. Functionally, these props became the working spaces needed for the office to operate. Smaller items are used to denote the town's outside space: typically, AstroTurf becomes a notional football pitch, accompanied by picnic tables, picket fences and hedges. This inner world is accessorized with kitsch ornaments – a large greyhound figurine, garden gnomes, a ceramic white rabbit and a bust of Lenin; even the lifeguard's tower has a striped lifeguard's ring, all treasured finds that further embellish the interior.

Narrative

Taste is rarely questioned in architecture, but the work of FAT is unusual in that it addressed this very issue. FAT eschewed traditionally accepted notions of architectural good taste. Instead, they embraced populist post-modern concerns of the everyday, of collage, of high versus low culture, even of bad taste. The props are residential in scale, familiar even, but their positioning within the chapel interior creates a strange world of contrasts, of a secular townscape located within a sacred chapel in the conscious recreation of a suburban set piece.

By taking the ordinary and playing with its scale and context, they create a series of dual meanings; surreal humour is at work here and it is an interior that brings a smile to your face with a clear nod to artist Marcel Duchamp's 'readymades'. Duchamp famously explored how everyday manufactured objects could be given new meaning within a different context, typically, that of the gallery. Context informs meaning and FAT have clearly developed a narrative that plays with the everyday but transforms its meaning through situation. Unexpected combinations create a hidden, introverted interior mise-en-scène formed as a kitsch post-modern stage set within a church, and it is this surreal jolt that psychologically makes it successful. This reminds the reader that props can be carefully chosen or designed to engender a sense of the unexpected.

Figures 4.15, 4.16 and 4.17 Kesselskramer, Amsterdam, Netherlands, 1998, designed by FAT. The selection of props within this interior, from habitable rooms disguised as notional miniature buildings through to the use of kitsch accessories, evokes a surreal yet humorous set piece. The playful juxtaposition of the props against the historic church interior allows meaning to be questioned.

4.17

Conclusion

This chapter aimed to facilitate your understanding of interior props in line with the chapter focus. The four categories of accessories, furniture, fixtures, and equipment are used to simply group, and illustrate, how these props could be central to staged space. The question being pondered related to if, or even how, interior props could enhance atmosphere, and whether they reinforced the idea of an interior mise-en-scène. French philosopher Jean Baudrillard's (1929–2007) seminal work on semiotics, originally published in 1968, introduced the concept of products as props that reinforced a consumer's lifestyle. For him, these products became 'sign-objects',[17] imbued with a secondary narrative, or meaning, that far exceeded their more prosaic utilitarian or financial value. This stance parallels the thinking in this chapter as it hopes to reveal the narrative value conceptually, spatially, aesthetically and psychologically pertaining to the use of interior props.

The refurbishment of the Ace Hotel by Roman and Williams and FAT's design for Kesselskramer's office both explore meaning through storytelling. Through the careful curation of vintage, flea-market and custom-made accessories, furniture and fixtures, Roman and Williams evocatively use props to capture a particular era or ambience. Similarly, FAT utilized a set of objects that were designed to evoke a notional townscape, in reality, carefully placed habitable props that reinforced the brand of the agency. A questioning of meaning through taste was an issue close to FAT's heart and in their surreal story of a former Catholic church, now populated by props that suggest a 'gigantic playground for adults'[18] (Kesselskramer, n.d.), it is clearly apparent. Evidently, a carefully styled interior can tell a story, or suggest a location, or a period, and this is an approach common to the world of production design. Roman and Williams would be familiar with this concept, and this approach imbues the Ace Hotel's interior with a sense of manufactured history that enhances its historic character.

Both Kubrick's *A Clockwork Orange* and Maggie's Cancer Caring Centres explore the psychological impact of space atmospherically. Kubrick's filmic interiors are useful in any discussion of extreme atmospheres; if Maggie's Cancer Caring Centres aim to emit a welcoming mood, then this cinematic interior is surely its polar opposite. The psychological aspect of the interior is often overlooked in the rush to create a visually beautiful setting. The disposition of interior props formed by the fetish mannequins stoked the fires of feminism, and perhaps it was not so much the nudity but how they were utilized in a clearly derogatory, subservient manner that rankled. Interiors that set out to be uncomfortable undoubtedly court controversy, and it is the recognition of unsettling societal mores that can enable the designer to develop disconcerting atmospheres for, say, branded interiors or event spaces.

Maggie's Cancer Caring Centres developed from a need to establish a base for a community of people who had either been diagnosed with cancer, or were supporting somebody through their illness and treatment. From the start, the design of the centres was to be the antithesis of your typical healthcare environment. Alongside a supportive community and a programme of events and workshops, these spaces aim to exude a welcoming, cosy and friendly atmosphere that psychologically invites you in. Fixtures that recall the familiar spaces of the home aim to psychologically disarm, and this suggests how familiar, even stereotypical, interior props (in this instance, a kitchen) can be used within another context because of the symbolic message they emanate. This approach embraces the archetypal meaning of the house previously discussed through the work of Bachelard (1958).

Finally, Landy's Break Down beautifully illustrates the dominant role that equipment re-imagined as an interior prop can take. The inclusion of equipment raises interesting questions regarding the role of spectacle, through performance, that certain types of interior props engender. For Landy, this was all about a theatre of destruction, complete with a noisy soundtrack and a busy workforce. This inhabited sense of space brings activity and noise to the fore, suggesting that interior atmosphere must acknowledge the sensory engagement of industry and a populated environment in the creation of an interior mise-en-scène. This grouping of case study conclusions simply aims to illustrate to the reader how interior props can inform atmosphere both aesthetically and psychologically, by underlining their role as an integral ingredient of any mise-en-scène for the interior.

FURTHER READING – EXPLORING INTERIOR PROPS

This chapter set out to explore the role that interior props play in the creation of interior atmosphere. The further readings included aim to clarify for the reader how interior props can be used to set the scene, evoking a certain atmosphere through their careful inclusion and curation.

The Arcades Project by Walter Benjamin was published posthumously in the 1980s but was actually written between 1927 and 1940. It is viewed as a literary critique of Parisian city life. Of particular pertinence here is Benjamin's consideration of the interior as a form of bourgeois self-expression, articulated by the objects it contains and the traces they leave (see Chapter I – The Interior, The Trace, pp. 212–27).

Roman and Williams: Things We Made (2012), by Stephen Alesch and Robin Standefer, details their alluring interior mise-en-scène creations, an approach undoubtedly learnt through their involvement with film. Their cinematic appreciation of space develops spatial narratives through the use of carefully selected and created props and environments, an approach that results in fully realized 'fictional' staged spaces.

The System of Objects, by French philosopher Jean Baudrillard (1968), clearly articulates, through an analysis of consumerism and the consumed object, his thoughts on the proliferation of meaning that objects (via their status as signs) now enjoy.

5 Special effects

Interior space and experiences

The senses not only mediate information for the judgement of the intellect, they are also channels which ignite the imagination and articulate sensory thought.[1]

(Pallasmaa, 1996: 31)

Figure 5.1
Flying Ladies, 1932: Four of Daly's chorus girls are hoisted aloft on 'invisible' wires during a rehearsal for the pantomime *Mother Goose*.
An interior mise-en-scène can exploit special effects in the creation of environments that deliberately play with our perception of space.

5.1

Introducing interior special effects

Interiors are inherently deceptive as they can use their decorative layers to 'taint' our perception of any given space through implication, suggestion and evocation. By creating aesthetic illusions and sensory experiences, they conjure up out of thin air immersive atmospheres for us as the audience and as the users of that space. This trait corresponds to the psychological aspect of mise-en-scène previously outlined in Chapter One and begs the question, 'is it all just a matter of perception?'.

Perception is an intrinsically subjective experience; what we see and how we see or feel it differ for each of us, but that does not mean that we are not susceptible to certain pervasive moods. How many times have you walked into a quiet room such as a place of worship and immediately modulated your speech down? Whilst the hushed silence of a library could be said to speak volumes. This suggests that atmosphere remains an inherently shared experience, one that aims to convey a certain tone or mood through an all-encompassing, carefully stage-managed ambience. Designers by recognizing these traits can knowingly 'colour' our perception of space.

Special effects – perception and atmosphere

Theatrically derived 'tricks of the trade' have a long and illustrious tradition within interior design. False perspectives, painted illusions, the use of mirrors, fake environments, faux impressions, dry ice, through to the deliberate manipulation of scale can all be viewed as spatial 'special effects'. Interestingly, the French philosopher Jean Baudrillard highlighted 'architectural illusion' and the potential 'dramaturgy'[2] (1999: 174) of buildings through their use of the art and techniques of the theatre. The ability of the built environment, focusing in this instance on the interior, to utilize these effects and introduce a magical 'sleight of hand' is central to this chapter. This 'misdirection' clearly hopes to engender a sense of awe and wonder in the audience by harnessing the magic and spectacle of the stage and screen.

In contrast to this drama, an interior that is attuned to the senses offers a bodily (through touch, taste, smell and sound), not just visual, appreciation of space and this will be given due consideration. The writings of French phenomenological philosopher Maurice Merleau-Ponty (1908–61) emphasize corporeality through 'bodily situation'[3] (1964: 05). For him, this visceral interpretation is the most important aspect of human perception as this bodily immersion directly informs our understanding of the surrounding environment. For Italian philosopher Tonino Griffero, atmospheric perception 'is a matter of affective and corporeal conditions aroused in the subject by external situations'[4] (2014: 10). Awareness of the sensory impact of space is the key that unlocks an understanding of the audience's perception, suggesting it should be viewed as an everyday component of the lived experience. Within the context of special effects, these attributes are often exaggerated perceptually, linked to the performative aspect of sensory design, so the heightened awareness that is given to the sensory should be viewed as a key aspect of an interior mise-en-scène. This chapter concentrates upon developing an understanding of the shared subjective experiences that an interior can create through the 'effects' it utilizes.

Within this chapter perceptions of space will be loosely grouped around four categories, each of which will be discussed in more detail in the summary to follow and through the more comprehensive case studies in the latter half of this chapter. These four groupings are:

1. Illusory space;
2. Implied space;
3. Use of scale;
4. Sensory space.

A deeper understanding of a mise-en-scène for the interior will be achieved only if both its physical and psychological properties are considered simultaneously. Perception therefore becomes a key ingredient; the chosen precedents all aim to illustrate how our perception of space can be intentionally manipulated, its 'presentation' doctored. This just leaves the focus for this chapter to be introduced and it is as follows:

CHAPTER FOCUS

- An introduction to the role of 'special effects' within interior design.
- An exploration of design approaches that utilize special effects through the four categories of illusory space, implied space, use of scale, and sensory space.
- An investigation of perception and its role in informing an interior mise-en-scène.

Illusory space

Illusory space sets out to deceive the eye through the use of painterly or graphic techniques. We are all so familiar with the film world of 'computer-generated imagery' (CGI) that it is easy to forget the role of decoration in the desire to deceive. Theatrical interiors of the stage as well as set designs for film still use simple painted backdrops to conjure spatial depth and perspective, evoking a certain time and place, whilst decorators and painters are still employed to master certain paint effects in the creation of an atmosphere of illusion. A form of illusion commonly employed within interior design is *trompe l'œil*, a pictorial deceit that creates optical illusions that 'enhance' or 'augment' reality. The examples that follow all utilize *trompe l'œil* to enhance the experience of the interior and explore the overlap between the stage set and the interior 'stage'.

A useful starting point for this discussion is *The Imaginarium of Doctor Parnassus*, a Terry Gilliam film from 2009. This film offsets traditional theatrical scenography against slick cinematic computer imagery to suggest two opposing worlds. The film tells the story of a travelling theatre troupe and their 'imaginarium' – a magical mirror that, once entered, enhances your mental creativity. The world of the imaginarium is computer-generated in contrast to Doctor Parnassus' travelling theatre, which clearly has Victorian origins. Gilliam was inspired by Pollock's Victorian toy theatres, essentially a miniature facsimile created as pop-up cardboard cut-outs[5] (Pr Mammoth NYC, 2009). In a homage to this tradition, Gilliam's travelling theatre uses scenery created through the use of simple theatrical 'flats' (in reality, cut, painted boards arranged as layers) to convey the illusion of spatial depth. This theatrical device of painted, layered space readily translates to interior design.

This illusory theatricality can also be found within the interior. The country houses of Europe and their historic interiors have traditionally employed *trompe l'œil* to add gravitas to their palatial environs, whilst narrating historical or religious events pictorially. Blenheim Palace in Oxfordshire, England, is an eighteenth-century baroque building with spectacular state apartments, home to the Duke of Marlborough. The interior of the saloon, or state dining room, was painted by French artist Louis Laguerre. With its illusory painted perspectives suggesting architectural vistas, and its gallery of painted spectators overlooking the guests dining in the saloon below, the artist utilizes *trompe l'œil* to commemorate the Duke's victory at the Battle of Blenheim in 1704. This illusory homage uses decoration to impress, venerate and commemorate in a room that is designed as a deliberate showcase. Both these examples raise interesting questions relating to the role of illusion within interior design.

5.2

Figure 5.2
The Saloon at Blenheim Palace, England, painted in 1704, architect Sir John Vanbrugh, artist Louis Laguerre.
Illusory space – the use of *trompe l'œil* creates an illusory painted backdrop of people, architecture and landscape, a vista that transforms this interior into a space of conscious spectacle and visual special effects.

Implied space

An interior that is not fully formed but instead drops 'hints' spatially can also be viewed as illusory; as the audience, we can join the dots, grasp the bigger picture and jump to a conclusion. Working with simple recurring motifs very much in the tradition of the stage, this form of space is 'implied'. Implied space can be seen as just another form of illusion that utilizes carefully positioned elements to suggest spatial territory, through notional boundaries and edges. It is often permeable rather than solid, using outline and silhouette to great effect as the following examples will illustrate.

An installation by Italian artist Esther Stocker, exhibited at the Centre for Contemporary Non-Objective Art in Brussels, imposes proportional repetitive elements into an existing interior. The monochromatic space becomes implied via a series of rectilinear fragmented lines and broken outlines, fixed as spatial coordinates that play with the participant's perceptual impression of the interior. This begs the question of how suggestion can be utilized to create space and mark spatial territory minimally. Building on this idea, a simple Bang & Olufsen stand at the Milan annual design fair in 1999 works

5.3

Figure 5.3
Abstract Thought is a Warm Puppy, Brussels, Belgium, 2008, by artist Esther Stocker.
Implied space – Stocker implies interior space through a system of rhythmic, repetitive elements that notionally suggest space and spatial territory.

conceptually to suggest another approach to implied space. Commissioned by Droog Design but designed by Dutch exhibition designers TRAAST + GRUSON, the outline of an apartment was formed by a light metal frame that was coated with phosphorescent paint. The designers famously embed storytelling within their work, so the electronic products are presented through the story of a notional fictional home. Motion sensors detect visitors as they enter the space, and this activates the equipment, cleverly focusing our attention on the product, whilst evoking the domestic realm further. This is another clear example of the role the imagination can play (with minimal design 'triggers') in understanding space.

Use of scale

Another key ingredient central to any discussion concerned with spatial perception has to be that of scale, which deserves a category all of its own because it can be used to such dramatic effect. Within an interior, scale can be either oversized or undersized; whichever you choose, it is aiming to be consciously different from the human scale we are familiar with and come to expect. Typically, scale can be used to evoke humour through surreal juxtapositions, as the following description attests, or it can be psychologically unsettling, as the more detailed case studies included in the second half of this chapter will highlight.

The Dutch industrial designer Marcel Wanders is well known for his sense of humour and fantastical approach to design, which is clearly in evidence for the design of the Mandarina Duck flagship store in London. Working with a luxury Italian brand specializing in luggage and travel items, the interior is appropriately inspired by the famous fictional eighteenth-century traveller from *Gulliver's Travels*[6] (Wanders, 2008). Gulliver finds himself shipwrecked and captured by a miniature race of people in Lilliput. This play on scale is clearly in evidence as a bright-yellow Gulliver (in reality, an oversized mannequin), standing at

5.4

Figure 5.4
Play House with Bang & Olufsen, Milan, Italy, 1999, by TRAAST + GRUSON (now credited to ProArtsDesign and Eword Traast).
Implied space – the design of this exhibition is formed by a minimal outline or silhouette, enhanced by sensory triggers, which leaves room for the imagination to interpret the story of this space.

nearly seven metres tall, dominates the interior, making us empathize with Lilliput's petite residents. This example illustrates how scale can be utilized within an interior to influence our perception of space.

Sensory space

Some would argue that the study of interiors is inherently a visual medium, one purely concerned with aesthetics and style. But this is to misunderstand the discipline and ignore the power of the lived sensory experience – of actually being in a space. The senses relate to the bodily faculties that recognize and process sensation through our sense of sight, sound, smell, touch and taste. All of our senses come to the fore when we are required to do more than just passively gaze at a space. By recognizing the sensory potential of an interior, certain senses can be prioritized, begging the question: how can an interior engage with our sense of smell or hearing? When a particular

sense is exaggerated, this can change our perception of a given space, potentially skewing the whole experience. This requires a conscious shifting of position from what are generally regarded as the traditional elements of the decorated interior – paint, wallpaper and textiles – to more ephemeral or transitory ingredients, as will be illustrated by the following description.

Located in the Barbican, London, the extraordinary Rain Room by Random International harnessed interior atmosphere through a literal downpour, and played with the surreal contradictions of being in a torrential deluge of rain inside whilst not getting drenched. The senses are initially assaulted through the sound of pounding rain. However, the expected sensory experience of feeling the rain falling does not occur; it is as if you can dictate the weather. The artists used digital technology to create this effect via a series of three-dimensional tracking cameras that

**Figure 5.5
Mandarina Duck store, London, England, 2008, by Marcel Wanders.**
Use of scale – a theatrical play of scale through the use of a bright-yellow oversized mannequin dominates this interior, altering our perception of its spatiality, whilst simultaneously introducing a new literary narrative to the fashion brand.

mapped the location of your body, turning the rain nozzles on and off as you progressed through the installation. This example illustrates how the manipulation of our senses can engender delight through unexpected juxtapositions that question stereotypical interior conventions.

Examples of interior mise-en-scène and their special effects

The examples included in the second half of this chapter are once again deliberately wide-ranging, culled from the world of film, art and design. They include an analysis of cinematic staging, the decorative setting of a historic hotel, as well as two interesting examples of experiential design. All aim to highlight the illusory role of special effects and their relevance to the design of interiors. In this instance, examples of special effects are included that embrace exaggerated visual, olfactory or auditory effects, spatial illusions, alongside an epicurean sense of taste. This is a combination that, when applied to the study of interiors, suggests a rethinking of the typically described definition of interior decoration as one that purely relates to surface treatment.

For simplicity of structure, each case study in this chapter will typically analyse the upcoming precedents by using the familiar headings of context and narrative, with an additional emphasis on special effects. This will create an opportunity for an analysis of how an interior utilizes scale, illusory, implied or sensory notions of space to taint our perception of atmosphere, and enhance the psychological aspect of an interior mise-en-scène.

5.6

Figure 5.6
The Rain Room, London's Barbican Centre, England, October 2012–March 2013, by Random International. Sensory space – the sensory component of this interior delights in unexpected juxtapositions of the notion of an internal weather system and the sound of rain inside.

Case Study One: Implied space – *Dogville*, director Lars von Trier

I was also inspired to a degree by Bertolt Brecht and his kind of very simple, pared-down theatre. My theory is that you forget very quickly that there are no houses or whatever. This makes you invent the town for yourself, but more importantly, it makes you zoom in on the people.[7]

(von Trier, cited in Bainbridge, 2007: 145)

Context

Released in 2003, *Dogville*, directed by Lars von Trier, is interesting within the context of this chapter because of the film's minimal staging, and it is this mere 'suggestion' of space that has led to its inclusion. Within Danish cinema, von Trier is important as the instigator of a collective of directors who all adhere to a series of principles outlined in the 'Dogma 95' manifesto and its 'Vow of Chastity'. They were interested in a form of film-making that eschewed cinematic artifice through the use of digital special effects and post-production trickery; instead, they advocated a return to human values and stories.

The film's narrative explores the issue of Grace (played by Nicole Kidman), who arrives as a fugitive and seeks refuge in Dogville, a small, remote town in the Rocky Mountains. As the film unfolds, Grace, in return for her safe haven, is increasingly pressurized to offer 'services', a position that sees her exploited and abused both mentally and physically.

Use of special effects

Shot entirely on a closed sound studio, Dogville is implied through chalk outlines and the minimal use of props. A back-to-basics philosophy is clearly expressed through the stark staging of this film as the streets of the town are simply laid out like a map drawn onto the dark floor. The judicious placement of props within these chalked outlines, such as a partial store front, a bed, a chair, or a wood-burning stove, all aim to minimally imply how these spaces are inhabited by the characters in the film. This approach to the interior setting is an attempt to 'suggest', rather than to produce, an accurate reproduction of an American townscape.

Narrative

Many writers, on analysing this film, have commented on von Trier's use of a 'Brechtian' form of 'epic theatre'[8, 9] (ibid.: 144 and Simons, 2007: 140), and Brecht (1898–1956), a twentieth-century playwright, poet and theatre director with Marxist sympathies, is famous for his use of alienation effects. These techniques aim to remind the audience that they are watching a deliberate fiction by breaking the passive, empathetic cycle, questioning the status quo, and hopefully prompting action. When considered against this theatrical tradition, von Trier's minimal, unrealistic staging clearly seeks to alienate the audience. What this sparse, fictionally implied world aims to emphasize are the film's characters and their moral and ethical dilemmas, rather than distract through an elaborately realized setting. This example clearly illustrates how interior space, particularly its spatial territory and character, can be simply and effectively implied.

Figure 5.7
Dogville, 2003, director Lars von Trier.
This cinematic example highlights how the interior spaces of a small town can be minimally implied. The staging of space is achieved through chalked territorial outlines and carefully chosen props in an approach inspired by Brecht.

Case Study Two: Illusory space – La Maison Champs Elysées, Maison Martin Margiela

The ubiquity of trompe-l'œil motifs is an exquisite metaphor for the house's complex relationship to time and history.[10]

(Debo, curator of '20', the exhibition to celebrate twenty years of Maison Martin Margiela, 2008: 04)

Context

Located in an archetypal, historic, French mansion in Paris, commissioned by the Duchess of Rivoli and designed by the French architect Jules Pellechet in 1886, this building has recently been refurbished by Belgian fashion house Maison Martin Margiela as a hotel. Seventeen hotel suites and key public spaces such as the reception, restaurant, bar and smoking room were upgraded during the 2011 refurbishment.

Margiela has developed an approach to fashion that is often grouped under the 'deconstructivist' epithet. This philosophical stance is realized through a conscious rethinking of the established systems concerned with the manufacturing, presentation and marketing of fashion. This approach is clearly in evidence through this case study and it has been included because it rethinks decoration as an illusory special effect.

5.8

Use of special effects

Margiela famously dissect and reconstruct old garments, materials and 'found' objects into new articles of clothing. This reverence for the old is also apparent in their 'replica' range where vintage clothes are cloned as exact copies. 'Time'[11] (ibid.: 08) conceptually remains central to their *oeuvre*, and this stance informs their approach to the interior renovation. Their own retail interiors famously utilize *trompe l'œil* as a recurring motif.

The hotel refurbishment intriguingly develops an illusory dialogue between the historic and original, or the theatrical or faux. Wherever possible, historical features are retained but these are juxtaposed against recently applied decorative deceits. Central to this concept is the historic Gilded Salon on the second floor with its beautiful French period gilt wall panelling. This interior is conceptually reconstructed through photography. Original period architectural features become transformed graphically into black-and-white photographic images, forming the *trompe l'œil* architectural wallpaper that lines the renovated interior.

5.9

Figures 5.8, 5.9, 5.10 and 5.11 **La Maison Champs Elysées, Paris, France, 2011, by Maison Martin Margiela.** The traditional decorative techniques of *trompe l'œil* are updated graphically as a series of black-and-white architectural photographs. These photographs become paper and textile liners in the hotel bedrooms that add illusory faux-decorative detail to a period property. Figure 5.11 illustrates the origins of the *trompe-l'œil* wallpaper – the historic Gilded Salon still located within the host building.

5.10

Narrative

The hotel's narrative is concerned with fictionalizing its past decoratively, but undertaking this with the surreal touch that this fashion house is renowned for.

Rather than just copying and reproducing the existing details, they instead opt to employ a graphic device that suggests decorative illusion. The ten *trompe-l'œil* bedrooms add architectural photographic detail to the walls and ceilings, whilst the floor rugs extend this idea graphically. This has allowed them to rethink the old, through a conscious splicing of the old with the new. This is a useful example of an interior mise-en-scène that plays with the traces of the past, of notions of time and illusion through its 'predilection for faux-ancient interiors'[12] (Dercon, 2008: 136–7), whilst highlighting how special effects can be introduced decoratively.

5.11

Case Study Three: Sensory space – Fragrance Lab for Selfridges, Campaign, The Future Laboratory and Givauden

The customer's physical presence and responses to stimuli and questions inform the alchemy of the fragrance to offer a meaningful, multi-sensory and customised consumer experience.[13]

(Campaign, 2015)

Context

Fragrance Lab was a temporary pop-up retail experience for one of London's premier department stores – Selfridges. Designed collaboratively, Selfridges worked alongside design studio Campaign, trend-forecasting agency The Future Laboratory, and perfumer Givauden to develop a concept that offered perfume as an immersive experience. This culminated in a personalized perfume, designed in response to the question: 'Can one's character be distilled into a scent?'. By prioritizing our sense of smell as a means for both navigating and characterizing interior space, this case study rightly earns its place in this chapter.

Figures 5.12, 5.13 and 5.14 **Fragrance Lab, a pop-up experience for Selfridges, 2014, London, England, developed by Campaign, The Future Laboratory, and Givauden.** This retail experience prioritizes our sense of smell as a journey through a series of aromatic encounters or special effects, suggesting that the sensory can replace the decorative in the staging of space.

5.12

Use of special effects

Located on the ground floor of the department store, the design expressed itself as an olfactory journey woven through a series of rooms, including part of the store's shop window. The customers became real-life shop mannequins, literal actors on a stage, offering a tantalizing glimpse – to the shoppers on the streets outside – of the event unfolding inside. Conceived as a sensory route, the tour began in a clinical, white, laboratory-style space with pseudo lab-coated technicians. These technicians guided you to an iPad where you were asked to respond to a series of images and statements. You were then issued with an audio guide, whilst a running commentary urged you into a series of spaces where you encountered different aromas. Between each encounter the smell of coffee beans was used to neutralize the palate. This journey continued into the shop window where you discovered a series of copper funnels filled with ingredients, emerging out of a mist of dry ice. The final space was designed to suggest a dispensary where your scent 'prescription' was discussed.

5.13

Narrative

The mise-en-scène of this interior is clearly driven by your sense of smell and this becomes its defining narrative, physically forming a journey of odour-filled encounters. By cleverly disguising psychometric tests as part of the experience, information on the customer and their shopping preferences are collated for the client. This psychological profile, along with your recorded scent preferences, helps to determine your signature scent developed by French perfumer Givauden. This personalized retail encounter aims to entice the customer back onto the shop floor; Philip Handford, the Creative Director of Campaign, usefully summarizes their immersive approach:

'what I'm imagining is retail as a form of theatre … It might start online, but what you get in-store would be an involving, visceral experience'[14] (Handford, cited in Kucharek, 2012).

By clearly illustrating how an appreciation of the sensory can result in an encounter that becomes a staged experience akin to a performance, this example highlights the starring role that can be given to the sensory.

5.14

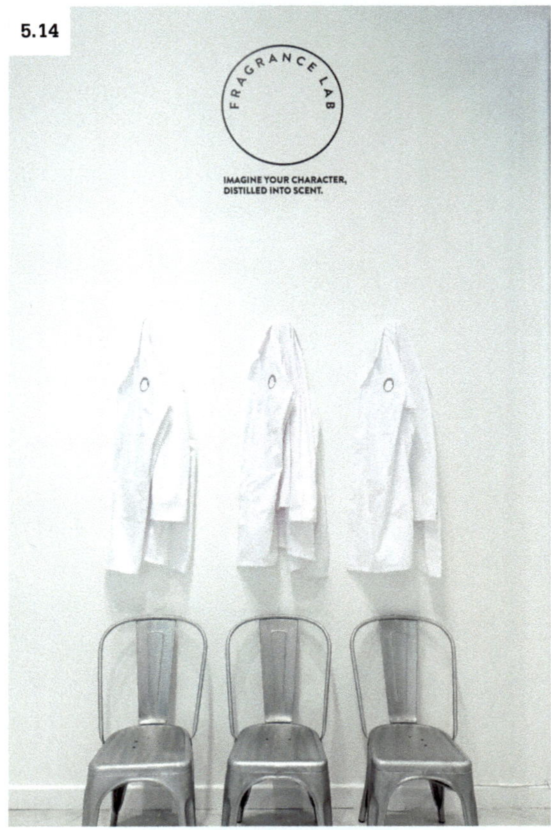

Case Study Four: Use of scale – *Citizen Kane*, director Orson Welles

Rolls of black velvet were hung in the empty spaces, causing them to register photographically as extreme depth. The result is a very sophisticated piece of optical trickery: the eye continually reads more than it actually sees.[15]

(Carringer, 1985: 62)

Context

Directed, produced by and starring Orson Welles (1915–85) and released in 1941, *Citizen Kane* remains influential, largely because of its technical prowess and its innovative approach to the staging of cinematic space. The story centres on the rise and fall of Kane, a fictional newspaper magnate, said to be inspired by the real life of American newspaper tycoon and movie mogul William Randolf Hearst (1863–1951).

The film sets, notionally under the control of Van Nest Polglase, were actually designed by Perry Ferguson, and it is the collaborative work of Welles, Ferguson and cinematographer Greg Toland that elevated the much-celebrated mise-en-scène of this film to something extraordinary. Venerated for its use of 'deep focus', a technique that resulted in both the foreground and the background being in simultaneous focus, the sets and how they were framed were able to suggest a gargantuan scale. It is the sense of scale developed as a special effect that is central to this case study's inclusion.

Use of special effects

The interior of 'Xanadu', especially its Great Hall, represents Kane's palatial fictional home. Inspired by Hearst's sprawling California estate 'San Simeon', Xanadu paid homage to its eclectic mix of architectural styles and priceless treasure trove of art and antiquities. As Carringer states in his comparative analysis of the two,

'the Hearstian element is brought out in the almost perverse juxtaposition of incongruous architectural styles and motifs'[16]

(ibid.: 54).

The interior deliberately plays with our perception of space, achieved through the use of low camera angles, wide-angle lens, and deliberately oversized props (the fireplace epitomizes this). The placement of the characters in relation to each other and bespoke optical tricks complement this scene. An attempt to control the spiralling film budget resulted in the set being partially built. Props and accessories, where possible, were recycled from previous productions; furniture was sparse. Parts of the set were left bare, swathed in black velvet and only partially lit. This added to the sense of scale as the room (and its ceilings) literally disappeared into the gloom. The scale of the Great Hall is further enforced by the deliberate echo that can be heard in the raised voices of the characters as they converse and pace across its empty expanse.

Narrative

As originally noted by Carringer[17] (ibid.: 55–6), the elimination of additional sets (another cost-cutting measure) resulted in the domestic life of Xanadu becoming centred in the ceremonially scaled, vast, empty space of the Great Hall. The contrast between the human figures and this space is extreme and the film's framing exaggerates this further. Narratively, this set came to represent symbolically the disintegration of the Kanes' marriage, as well as their increased isolation. The design of the Great Hall was dictated as much by financial constraints as it was by creative endeavour, but the result is a psychologically challenging mise-en-scène that understands how to use scale to optimum effect. It aims to highlight how the deliberate exaggeration of scale through 'optical trickery' and exaggerated acoustics can contribute towards a specific interior mood.

Figure 5.15
***Citizen Kane,* 1941, director Orson Welles.** Cinematically, *Citizen Kane* plays with a scale that dwarfs its inhabitants; the powerful composition, alongside visual and auditory tricks, helps to evoke further the supposed grandeur of the fictional Xanadu through a combination of special effects.

Case Study Five: Sensory space – Alcoholic Architecture, Bompas & Parr

Vaporizing the cocktail seemed to heighten the flavour for an ultra-intense G&T experience … All the while, the alcohol was being absorbed via the lungs and even the eyeballs.[18]

(Bompas & Parr, 2010: 151)

Context

Bompas & Parr are a British-based duo of self-styled food alchemists. Their design studio is an interesting mix of designers, cooks and architects, all of whom collaborate on 'flavour-based experience design'[19] (Bompas & Parr, 2015). Famous for their culinary experiments with jelly, their past repertoire has included fireworks you can smell, as well as scratch 'n' sniff film cards. Their pop-up experience titled Alcoholic Architecture aimed to 'create a walk-in cloud of breathable cocktail'[20] (Bompas & Parr, 2010: 152), a novel interpretation of literally 'soaking up the atmosphere'. The resultant interior is included as a case study because it explores sensory design by introducing taste as an experiential component of atmosphere.

Use of special effects

For this project the sense of taste dominated its evolution. By creating an immersive cloud of gin and tonic, a fog that you literally walked into, Bompas & Parr transformed a simple drink with your friends into a shared sensory experience. For them, the act of taste becomes 'externalised' and re-imagined on an architectural scale[21] (Jacob, 2009). The event to date has had two incarnations in London, the original in Soho in 2009, whilst the second and most recent in Borough, an area with a rich history of gastronomic and alcoholic delights. This intense sensory experience involved descending into a basement, donning a plastic poncho, before emerging into a dense alcoholic fog (in essence, a vaporized cloud of gin and tonic) with a liquor-to-mixer ratio of 1:3 and a humidity level of 140 per cent. The fog was unexpectedly chill, damp, disorientating even, blurring the spatial boundaries and partially obscuring other punters, exacerbated by the use of flashing lights and pulsing music. Customers were limited to fifty minutes, roughly the equivalent in bodily absorption of one strong drink whilst a sign encouraged you to 'breathe responsibly'.

5.16

5.17

Narrative

Alcoholic Architecture is concerned with exploring taste as a defining narrative of design. As designers, or as users of space, we regularly find ourselves discussing what a space looks like or what it feels like, or even sounds like through its acoustic qualities, but how often do we discuss what it might taste like? Bompas & Parr place this often-overlooked sense centre stage in the development of a mise-en-scène that is gastronomic. For them, interior atmosphere is utilized as an 'effect', that of a vapour cloud that we can taste, feel (through its cool temperature) and see simultaneously. This raises interesting questions regarding the consideration of the senses within the design of interiors. The ability of Bompas & Parr to cross-design genres suggests that there is room for both flavour and feel as a consideration of the bodily experience of interior atmosphere.

5.18

Figures 5.16, 5.17 and 5.18 **Alcoholic Architecture, London, England, 2015–16 by Bompas & Parr.** This 'walk-in' cocktail envelopes its audience in a chilled cloud of vaporized gin and tonic, prioritizing our sense of taste as an intense interior experience and special gastronomic effect.

Conclusion

This chapter aims to establish whether our initial impressions of interior space can be affected by the way it has been formed perceptually and presented to its audience. The four headings of illusory space, implied space, sensory space, and the use of scale attempt to initially group, and then distil, design approaches that utilize these interior special effects. As with previous chapters, the included design precedents serve as an introduction, and exploration, of this approach to interior design. Within the concept of an interior mise-en-scène, the notion of spectacle is a recurring theme, and this potentially elevates the performative qualities of an interior. The question of perception leads us to the crux of the matter, and the conclusions are addressed here.

Dogville, La Maison Champs Elysées and *Citizen Kane* all share an approach perceptually that plays with spatial illusion. This interior characterization is clear in the cinematic staging of *Dogville* and its employment of implied space. Through the use of minimal props and mere outline, it manages to evoke a spartan townscape. This townscape is based upon imaginative suggestion, rather than on a meticulously recreated architectural simulacrum that is presented as a fait accompli. In contrast, La Maison Champs Elysées illustrates how *trompe l'œil*, in a clear homage to the original period architectural features, can be used to enhance a historic interior through the addition of illusory decoration. This special effect transforms the interior (typical of many hotels) into a carefully orchestrated staged encounter as the setting revels in its scenic role, reflecting the fashion

brand of Maison Martin Margiela. Meanwhile, *Citizen Kane* illustrates how ideas from film concerning scale, enhanced through the use of light and shadow and deliberately echoing acoustics, could be more fully exploited when considering the designed impression of an interior. Such an interior atmosphere can consciously embrace the brooding as well as the convivial. These three examples serve to illustrate the notion of deliberate artifice, of a designed interior that embraces a sense of the dramatic by utilizing spectacle as a constituent ingredient. This is an approach that is echoed in the writings of German philosopher Gernot Böhme and his aligning of manufactured atmosphere to key elements of stage design (2013).

In contrast, the remaining two case studies clearly exploit our perception of space through our senses. Selfridges' Fragrance Lab highlights how the prioritizing of smell can lead to an interior that is driven by olfactory concerns. Meanwhile, the walk-in cocktail of Bompas & Parr creates an interior experience that prioritizes our sense of taste – a fug of atmosphere that becomes simultaneously seen, felt and tasted. Both examples underline the benefit of expanding the current rather-restricted view of decorated space to one that consciously encompasses the whole gamut of sensory phenomena. This stance is echoed in the writings of architectural theorist Juhani Pallasmaa and his belief that atmosphere is understood through 'peripheral perception'[22] (Pallasmaa, 2014: 38), established through a continual scanning of our senses. By considering the power of perception, presentation and the role of special effects, the interior becomes the location for a staged encounter. This approach, alongside the other chapter case studies, correlates to the concept of staged space already outlined in this book. Together, they display an uncanny ability to enhance atmosphere through a bodily appreciation of space, surely a key consideration in the creation of a mise-en-scène for the interior.

FURTHER READING – CONSIDERING SPECIAL EFFECTS

Interior special effects are utilized to visually transform space through optical tricks – tricks that play with scale, or evoke illusions, or suggest through implication certain spatial territories or characteristics. The decision to include the sensory within this chapter prompted a reconsideration of special effects as something that can move beyond the purely visual to one that embraces smell, or taste, or the tactile or aural qualities of the interior. In all cases, the resultant mise-en-scène directs the user's response through the simple exaggeration of the inherent experiential quality of interior space. Further readings relating to this topic are included below for the interested reader.

New Realism in Film Architecture (2000) by Eric Hanson, a digital film designer in Bob Fear's A.D. Architecture + Film II, chronicles the history of cinematic special effects. He charts the transition from traditional theatrically derived built sets, through filming techniques, to today's extensive use of digital technology.

'Space, Place and Atmosphere: Peripheral Perception in Existential Experience', by Juhani Pallasmaa in *Architectural Atmospheres: On the Experience and Politics of Architecture* (2014), editor Christian Borch, succinctly reinstates Pallasmaa's belief that atmospheric perception is experienced both emotionally and as a multi-sensory encounter.

The Primacy of Perception, by Maurice Merleau-Ponty, with this English edition from 1964 (editor James M. Edie), clearly sets out this philosopher's thoughts on perception. Chapter One contains a previously unpublished text that explores Merleau-Ponty's concept of 'bodily situation' with regard to understanding space.

6 Light and shadow

Uncovering its dramatic role

This was the genius of our ancestors, that by cutting off the light from this empty space they imparted to the world of shadows that formed there a quality of mystery and depth superior to that of any wall painting or ornament.[1]

(Tanizaki, [1933] 1977: 20–1)

Introducing light and shadow

Light is multifaceted as it can be seen to have functional, aesthetic and psychological properties. It can enhance the interior setting by radically altering its mood and affecting our perception of any given space. Interiors can be designed to knowingly entice you in, their beacons of light suggesting a refuge of conviviality and warmth in stark contrast to the dark, deserted streets outside and their pools of intense, intimidating shadows. Light and shadow are all-pervasive; they envelop us, they conceal and reveal, invite you in, or repel you and put you on your guard – a concept that the interiors of film are familiar with and exploit. Cinematographers are central to this process as their technical proficiency can enhance these qualities. Light is also directional, creating areas of spotlight in stark contrast to their corresponding shadows; light also has a functional quality as certain activities require a specific level of light. The duration of the day is marked by the move from natural to artificially lit interiors, so light, in all of its many guises, has always characterized the inner world of the interior. This leads us to the focus for this chapter, which can be summarized as follows:

> **CHAPTER FOCUS**
>
> - An introduction to the role of 'light and shadow' within interior design.
> - An exploration of design approaches that utilize these ingredients through the four categories of natural, artificial, candle, and digital light.
> - An investigation of the psychological aspect of light and shadow and its role in the creation of a mise-en-scène for the interior.

Lighting and atmosphere

Within this chapter, light and shadow will be loosely grouped into four categories, each of which will be discussed in more detail in the summary below and in the more comprehensive case studies that follow. These four groupings are:

1. Natural light;
2. Artificial light;
3. Candlelight;
4. Digital light.

Figure 6.1
'Studio Portrait', Swedish–American actress Greta Garbo (1905–90) as Irene Guarry during filming of the romantic drama *The Kiss*, directed by Jacques Feyder.
Light and shadow have always been central to the creation of interior atmosphere, important because they have the potential to taint psychologically any interior mise-en-scène.

The chosen precedents aim to illustrate how the use of light and shadow within an interior setting can contribute towards, and enhance, a particular mood. This chapter concentrates upon the 'effect' of light in the creation of interior atmosphere rather than on its technical specification. The focus is upon exploring the role of light as one of the key psychological elements in a mise-en-scène for the interior.

Natural light

Interiors can be flooded with natural light through the disposition of openings within the physical fabric of the building, or they can be shuttered, closed to the light, belonging to the realm of shadows. Natural light, which can also be referred to as daylight, can be channelled, directed within the interior by physical light shafts, filters or apertures until the desired effect is achieved. Light can be coloured, tainted by the physical colour or material it touches or passes through. The consideration of 'aspect' can also have a real impact and this relates to the orientation of a building, for example, its 'southerly aspect'. By referencing the cardinal points of the compass – north, south, east and west – you can start to understand that each has its own particular quality of light relating to the temporality of the day. All of these factors can transform space. The following descriptions aim to illustrate the use of natural light and shadow within an interior.

James Turrell has spent all of his life harnessing the effects of natural and artificial light within a variety of environments. His 'Skyscapes' are simply purpose-built spaces that frame and focus attention on the sky through an open portal by offering different modes of seeing. They create atmospheric incident within a plain setting through openings that channel light occurrences as they traverse the interior. This atmosphere dramatically changes as the day draws to a close through the use of a preprogrammed, artificial light show that perceptually challenges the viewer's experience of the

Figure 6.2
A 'Skyscape' light installation, Albion Barn, Oxford, England, 2014, by artist James Turrell.
Natural light – the 'Skyscape' that Turrell temporarily installed at Albion Barn for Michael Hue-Williams uses natural light and sky views to animate a simple interior chamber, whilst the night sky becomes enhanced by a coloured artificial light display.

unfolding celestial panorama. This suggests that light can be used to literally 'decorate' a space. The temporary installation of a Skyscape at Albion Barn, a former farm, since renovated by studio Seilern Architects into an arts centre for international gallery owner Michael Hue-Williams, beautifully illustrates the power of light to animate interior space.

The decorative – or perhaps it would be more appropriate to say the atmospheric – qualities of light and shadow are well used in film. Film noir as a genre is famous for its use of shadows cinematically, harnessed to conjure psychologically oppressive atmospheres. Closely associated with the amoral American crime dramas from the forties and fifties, these films concentrated upon the dark underbelly of society by examining themes of exploitation, sexual tension, and corruption, presented via a highly stylized, brooding mise-en-scène. This is exemplified by Billy Wilder's (1906–2002) 1944 film, *Double Indemnity*, starring Barbara Stanwyck as Phyllis Dietrichson, the femme fatale who plots to murder her husband for an insurance payout. Director of photography John F. Seitz contrasted the bright sunlight of the Californian exteriors against the shadowy, unkempt interior of duplicitous Dietrichson's house, pierced only by the occasional shaft of daylight. Aluminium particles were deliberately blown in front of the camera to emulate dust motes cinematically, whilst venetian blinds were used to create dramatic horizontal shadows across the faces and bodies of the guilty protagonists to subtly imply imprisonment[2] (Phillips, 2010: 62–3). Both these lighting devices suggest this phenomenon can be invested with subtle meaning.

A further understanding of the meaning that lighting strategies can attain can be found in the work of modernist architect Le Corbusier. He delivered a masterclass in the use of natural light in the design for his Chapel of Notre Dame du Haut, located in Ronchamp, France. Completed in 1955, this Catholic interior is dark and cavernous, topped by a heavy roof that compresses the interior space, yet the light emotes, communicating a deeper, spiritual meaning that uses aspect to great effect. The thick wall of the southern façade is interspersed with myriad openings, illuminating the stained glass that is sprinkled liberally along its length. This glass taints the light as it enters the interior, creating pools of reflected colour that glow within the dark interior. The east wall behind the altar captures the morning light through small piercings suggestive of stars, whilst an effigy of Our Lady sits within a glazed box that becomes, appropriately, suffused with a halo of light. Le Corbusier strived to create a space full of spiritual nuance, and this approach illustrates how a designer aware of symbolic meaning can harness the qualities of light and shadow as an expressive medium.

Artificial light

Artificial light, which can also be referred to as electric light, offers different qualities of 'ambient' light. This is the light that envelops and surrounds us, aiming to communicate a general impression or mood. This mood can be characterized by a clinical brightness, neon exuberance, shadowy mystery, or be determined by the choice of light fitting. Artificial light can inform the legibility of space by suggesting arrival, marking movement by highlighting navigable corridors and paths, as well as helping to define the interior spatially or hierarchically. Available in a rainbow spectrum of colour choices, light can emulate daylight, add colour to an interior, offer a range of lux levels (lux is a unit of illumination), whilst the light glow it emanates can be warm or cold, bright or dull, as the situation requires. The intensity of artificial light results in shadows that can be determined, working in contrast to artificially spotlighted shafts of light, an approach that is highlighted in the following description.

A former industrial warehouse in Mumbai, India, becomes the location for a series of recording studios and an acoustic lounge consisting of a restaurant, bar and music stage. Designed by Serie Architects, a series of artificially back-lit, glowing, acrylic, circular, resin dining booths offer the primary light source within this dark interior. These booths are cleverly terraced to allow uninterrupted site lines to the stage. This interior through the design of its fixtures is characterized by its evocative use of shadow, an approach that beautifully captures the qualities of a night-time venue suggesting that a deliberately under-lit interior can enrich atmosphere.

Figure 6.3
The BlueFROG Music Club, Mumbai, India, 2007, by Serie Architects.
Artificial light and shadow – artificially produced light and shadow imbue this deliberately dark venue with an arresting interior atmosphere, an ambience that clearly values the inherent mystery of shadows.

6.3

Candlelight

Candlelight is light that is neither natural nor artificial (in the sense that it is not powered by electricity). Instead, it is light that has its origins in the open fires, lamps and candles that historically illuminated interiors. It is often overlooked as a light source in an age where light is expected at the flick of a switch, but its consideration and inclusion bathe interiors in a softer glow, whilst relegating a room's periphery to the shadows. The following description aims to illustrate the use of candlelight within an interior.

Stanley Kubrick's 1975 period film *Barry Lyndon* famously utilized candlelight for the interior scenes. Based on the 1844 novel by William Makepeace Thackeray, the film charts the rise and subsequent fall of an Irish adventurer (the hero of the title). Working with cinematographer John Alcott, and legendary production designer Ken Adam, Kubrick was inspired by period paintings and aimed to translate their painterly use of light onto the big screen[3] (Howard, 1999: 140–1). Filmed entirely on location, utilizing a series of heritage properties, the glow of isolated candelabras within a shadowed room aimed to recreate authentically the mood of an eighteenth-century interior, captured via a series of bespoke camera lenses. This example aims to highlight the role of lighting as a device that communicates by evoking a specific time and place, investing the whole interior with a specific ambience.

6.4

Figure 6.4
***Barry Lyndon,*
1975, director
Stanley
Kubrick.**
Candlelight – the reliance upon candlelight whilst filming caused endless technical problems but it captured beautifully a period interior of soft light, surrounded by encroaching shadows.

Digital light

Digital light conceives of light as an effect characterized by moving imagery. This type of light is often concerned with narrative, animating space through the use of an illuminated backdrop. It transfers digital technology into the world of the interior, consciously blurring the physical world of a building with the digital world of animation and film. These relationships are often site-specific, one-off, custom-made interior adventures that become immersive digital experiences. The use of digital light sets out to create interiors of spectacle and incident, as illustrated by the following description.

'Soft Sell', an early work by New York-based Diller + Scofidio (now Diller, Scofidio + Renfro), introduced video to the Rialto Theatre on 42nd Street. An abandoned porn theatre played host to an installation that toyed with our understanding of desire. A pair of over-scaled, luscious, red lips tempted passers-by with a series of verbally provocative offers relating to consumerism, whilst cleverly referencing the previous sleazy location. Light in this instance becomes linked to spectacle, is participatory, and this raises interesting questions regarding its relationship to its audience.

Figure 6.5
'Soft Sell', New York, USA, 1993, Diller + Scofidio.
Digital light – the use of film infuses this interior atmosphere with a sense of spectacle via an installation that utilizes an animated backdrop of light and moving imagery.

6.5

Examples of interior mise-en-scène – using light and shadow

For the Japanese author Tanizaki (introduced in Chapter One), his iconic ode to shadows is essentially a lament to a passing age – an age that, for him, was intent on eradicating the seductive mystery of gloom from daily life. His wholesale praise of dark interiors with their 'visible darkness'[4] ([1933] 1977: 35) becomes a useful point of departure for considering the phenomenon of light and shade within interior space. The cinematic interior reinforces this approach by raising interesting questions regarding the psychological interpretation of these ingredients. The examples included in the second half of this chapter are, once again, deliberately wide-ranging, gathered from the world of film, art and design, which encompass office, theatre and hotel interior genres. They have been selected because of the central role that light or shadow takes in the creation of interior atmosphere. Each case study will be analysed through the usual structure of context and narrative, whilst special attention is this time given to the use of light and shadow.

Case Study One: Shadow – *Nosferatu*, director F.W. Murnau

Art consists in eliminating. But in the cinema it would be more correct to talk of 'masking'. For just as you and Röhrig suggest light by drawing shadows, so the cameraman ought to create shadow too. That's much more important than creating light.[5]

(Murnau, cited in Eisner, remembered by Herlth, [1964] 1973: 62)

Context

This case study has been included because of its iconic use cinematically of shadow; within the history of film, German expressionism as a genre was an early exploiter of darkness. Shadow is clearly used to taint an interior psychologically in the creation of an unsettling atmosphere. *Nosferatu* takes advantage of both natural and artificial light to harness the role that shadow plays in conjuring a particular cinematic mood. Filmed in Germany in 1922, not long after the end of the First World War, the fledgling democratic Weimar Republic became an intense centre for artistic film-making. Inspired by the art of German expressionism, the films created and released during this period displayed an uncanny ability to visually convey psychologically unsettling cinematic imagery. Directed by F.W. Murnau (1888–1931), the film's complete title is *Nosferatu: A Symphony of Horror*. The film's screenplay was based on Bram Stoker's classic novel *Dracula* but a legal wrangle over copyright led to a change of name for the film. *Dracula* was substituted by a regional term for the undead – *Nosferatu*.

The use of light and shadow

Murnau is much admired as an early innovator within film. *Nosferatu*, even though it is a silent black-and-white film, is referenced as much for its technical proficiency as for its construction of an intense atmosphere through the use of contrasting light and shadow that came to be known as chiaroscuro. Murnau's cinematographer Fritz Arno Wagner helped to realize in celluloid his ideas. Much has been written concerning the German nation's innate love of *unheimlich* (a term Freud appropriated), and Roberts describes this beautifully in his book on German expressionism as

'the weird or uncanny, referring to an ill-defined sense of subconscious horror, latent spirits and repressed emotions'[6]

(2008: 13).

Unheimlich taints the approach to shadows; they literally become a malevolent force cinematically.

Narrative

Nosferatu, unusually for a German expressionist film, incorporated key locations into its narrative. As Eisner[7] ([1952] 1969: 101) noted, the medieval townscapes of the Baltic became Nosferatu's castle, and this location easily conveys a sense of the uncanny through its narrow, claustrophobic alleyways and naturally occurring intense pools of light and dark. Max Schreck, the actor playing Nosferatu, used costume and make-up to convey a particular impression of the vampire. Through this characterization, Nosferatu is deliberately repellent, which adds to the film's foreboding mise-en-scène, as his pale face emerges out of the darkness.

This sense of dread is further enhanced by shadow play. Nosferatu's shadow acts as a metaphor for death and disaster, a portent of doom; it becomes a character in its own right. This is clearly shown in scenes where the shadow cast by his creeping figure, with clawed hands, slowly and inevitably makes its way towards his chosen victim. His cast shadow even appears on their faces and bodies. This example is important to the study of interiors because it highlights how shadows, if employed successfully as an atmospheric device, can infect an ordinary, everyday interior with a narrative of extraordinary menace.

6.6

Figure 6.6
***Nosferatu*, 1922, director F.W. Murnau.**
The use of light and shadow in *Nosferatu* created the original cinematic Gothic blueprint. Shadows became central to the film's sense of impending dread, as ordinary interior spaces became 'infected' by Nosferatu's presence.

Case Study Two: Artificial light – 'The Weather Project', Olafur Eliasson

I consider the works as sort of 'phenomena-producers', like machines, or stage sets, producing a certain thing in a more or less illusory way.[8]

(Eliasson, cited in Birnbaum, 2002: 14)

Context

Olafur Eliasson is a Danish–Icelandic artist whose work harnesses natural phenomena such as light, rain, sun, wind and rainbows in the creation of immersive encounters that play with the senses. He refers to these ready-made landscapes as 'phenomena-producers' and he uses them to challenge the spectator's perception of space. 'The Weather Project' was temporarily installed in the Turbine Hall of the Tate Modern, London, in 2003 for six months. It became the meteorological event of the year, as a man-made weather system literally permeated the interior of the museum. This iconic example of Eliasson's work has been included because it beautifully illustrates how artificial light can moderate an existing interior environment.

The use of light and shadow

This project was composed of artificial lighting re-imagined to the scale of a landscape with a gigantic, glowing, yellow sun seen through a screen of artificial fog. This simulated environment sets out to explore whether the weather impacts upon our emotions. A questionnaire sent to the Tate staff by the artist included the question: 'To what extent do you find the weather affects your mood?', to which 59 per cent answered: 'it significantly affects my mood'[9] (May, 2003: 63). This undoubtedly explains the audience's response to the phenomenon as a space of entrancing spectacle before which they notionally sunbathed.

On closer inspection, this hazy miasma is revealed as a deliberate construct as the props that produced this effect are revealed to the spectator. The sun was formed by a half-circle of mono-frequency bulbs (more commonly used in street lighting), concealed behind a projection screen. This form of lighting reveals colours only as yellow or black, so that the interior becomes seen through a restricted colour filter. The ceiling was covered in mirrored tiles to convey the impression of a full circle of light, simultaneously doubling the scale of the space, whilst the apparatus that created the artificial mist was also exposed.

Figures 6.7 and 6.8 'The Weather Project', October 2003–March 2004, Tate Modern, London, England, by artist Olafur Eliasson. Artificial light in the hands of Eliasson becomes part of an evocative meteorological atmosphere of sun and mist that invaded atmospherically the space of the Tate Modern.

Narrative

Eliasson refers to this as 'seeing yourself seeing'[10] (Grynsztejn, 2007: 23) and it is concerned with a demystifying of the first impression. By revealing the atmosphere as one of deliberate artifice – a staged encounter – he reveals that our perception has been 'mediated'[11] (Eliasson, 2003: 133–5), which is an important recurring condition in Eliasson's work. At play here is a dual narrative of encounter and revelation that utilizes an artificially lit landscape of sun and mist to imbue the interior with a special atmospheric yellow aura. However, the spell is broken as it subsequently unmasks its own magic. This example encapsulates for any design student how light can completely transform space, whilst this engineered spectacle influences how its audience responds to the encountered interior mise-en-scène.

6.8

Case Study Three: Natural light – D.E. Shaw and Co. Offices, Steven Holl

The projected colors [*sic*] vary in saturation with the intensity of the sunlight on a given day. The movement of the sun enlivens the colors [*sic*] and transforms this time-movement into a strange and glowing flow.[12]

(Holl, in Holl, Pallasmaa and Pérez-Gómez, 2006: 61)

Context

Steven Holl is an American architect interested in the phenomenology of architecture, meaning that he prioritizes the subjective, poetic and sensory quality of the built environment. A significant proportion of his work explores the manipulation of light and its role in enhancing perceptually our impression of a given space. His design for the offices of D.E. Shaw and Co. encapsulates this approach in the creation of an ever-changing light show that transforms the physical fabric of the interior. This case study has been included because of this phenomenon.

D.E. Shaw, a financial trading company, currently occupies offices located on the top two floors of a skyscraper in Manhattan, New York. Completed in 1991, this iconic interior became famous for its ephemeral use of 'projected color' [*sic*][13] (ibid.: 61).

The use of light and shadow

By inserting a new skin into the existing interior, expressed as a simple, stretched cube, Holl creates a backdrop for an investigation of light. This cubic space forms the white reception volume characterized via a series of notched openings. These openings reveal a double layer formed by the original outer wall of the building and the new inserted cube wall, set within, and slightly back from, this original boundary. This cubic device controls the amount of natural light entering the interior. Light becomes indirect, seeping into the space to create incidents of brightness only where the openings dictate. The rear of this new cube is painted green, yellow and orange in bright, fluorescent colours and, even though this painted surface is hidden from view, its effect is clearly in evidence. It colours the light as it enters the interior creating a wash of reflected colour. By night the same effect is produced through the use of artificial light.

Narrative

For Holl, architecture comes to life when the physicality of the building and its interior collides with the world of sensory perception. Light, if harnessed appropriately, can invest an interior space with a particular mood, creating a narrative that can transform throughout the day as the quality of that light changes. Projected colour, or colour seen through light, is dematerialized; it glows, is ethereal rather than fixed. For Holl, it is this inherent unpredictability – its very transience alongside the 'transformative' qualities of light itself – that is attractive. This interior illustrates how the mysterious intersection of light and colour creates a perceptual mise-en-scène that suggests a 'psychological space' that has an 'emotive effect'[14] (Safont-Tria, 2012: 55). The production of an ever-changing light show transforms the physical fabric of the interior, highlighting how the consideration and inclusion of natural phenomena can enrich interior atmosphere.

6.9

6.10

**Figures 6.9 and 6.10
D.E. Shaw and Co. Offices, New York, USA, 1991–2 by architect Steven Holl.**
Holl experiments with the mysterious ever-changing phenomenon of 'projected colour'. This approach enhances interior atmosphere by using natural light to magically diffuse hidden colour into space, giving it an ephemeral character.

Case Study Four: Candlelight – Sam Wanamaker Playhouse – Allies and Morrison and Jon Greenfield

It's interesting that we use this phrase 'live flame' … it moves, it dances, it flickers … The great moment [in the Playhouse] is when the six chandeliers are suspended just above the stage.[15]

(Martin White, candle expert to the Playhouse, cited in Hemming, 2013)

Context

The recreated Globe Theatre, close to its original site on the banks of the River Thames, was one of the first purpose-built theatres in London. As the original location for many of his plays, it is the spiritual home to pre-eminent English poet and playwright, William Shakespeare (1564–1616). It was always intended that this rebuilt outdoor theatre would be complemented by an indoor Jacobean playhouse, allowing for all-year-round productions. Housed in a brick shell immediately adjacent to the reconstructed Globe, this space offers an alternative intimate, candlelit interior. The design was informed by drawings found in Worcester College Library in Oxford in 1964 that were later ascribed to architect Inigo Jones' protégé John Webb (1611–72) circa 1660. As one of the few contemporary instances of an interior that was designed to deliberately include candlelight, this example reveals how this ingredient can become integral to the resultant interior atmosphere.

6.11

Figure 6.11
The Sam Wanamaker Playhouse, Shakespeare's Globe Theatre, London, England, 2014, by Allies and Morrison, and Jon Greenfield.
A re-imagined seventeenth-century, indoor theatre recreates a candlelit interior in the quest for an authentic period atmosphere.

Use of light and shadow

Rather than being concerned with the recreation of a particular building, the indoor theatre is a re-imagining of an archetypal Jacobean playhouse interior that, if Shakespeare were still alive today and walked into, he would be familiar with. It needed to convey the spirit of the age by using authentic construction techniques, sympathetic materials and decoration, whilst offering an opportunity to stage the Bard's plays within an authentic context. The use of candlelight was central to the credibility of this atmosphere. Lit by wall sconces and by candelabra hung from the ceiling, the flickering light illuminates the interior, creating areas of light and shadow and an intimate all-encompassing atmosphere. The gilt work in the mythological scene hand-painted on the ceiling of the playhouse glitters in the gloom, whilst the light from the stage focuses your attention on the actors and the world they are creating.

Narrative

This re-imagined theatre not only recreates the atmosphere of a Jacobean playhouse, but also allows for an investigation into the seventeenth-century staging of Shakespeare's plays through the use of lighting, costume and music. The lighting already mentioned is complemented by candles held by actors. Candles become mobile, are blown out and relit for dramatic effect as they help to punctuate and illustrate the story being told; they reinforce the narrative. The rich interplay of candlelight and its resultant light and shadow became an integral aspect of the rebuild, largely because it was central to the recreation of the ambience of a specific period and the staging of its plays. It serves to highlight the role this type of lighting can undertake in the enhancement of an interior mise-en-scène.

Figure 6.12
Actors Joseph Marcell, Richard Bremmer and Kevin Moore perform in *The Inn at Lydda* at The Sam Wanamaker Playhouse in London in September 2016. Candlelight enhances the performance and stagecraft and is central to the production.

Case Study Five: Digital light – The West Lobby in The Cosmopolitan, Rockwell Group's LAB

We think about choreographing environments.[16]

(Tichenor and Walton, 2012)

Context

The Rockwell Group is an innovative design practice based in New York led by architect David Rockwell. They are well known for their creative problem-solving defined by Rockwell's famous 'What If …?' philosophy and theatrically informed approach to design. LAB, a key aspect of the practice, is a technologically inquisitive research team that aims to explore the intersection of the 'digital and physical realms'. The West Lobby, located in The Cosmopolitan hotel, Las Vegas, became the location for an extraordinary digital environment that aimed to capture the notion that 'people go to Las Vegas for an experience they're not going to get in their hometowns'[17] (Rockwell, 2014: 305). This case study has been included as an example of how digital light not only overcomes a problematic site, but also augments a bland interior in the creation of a transformative experience for its hotel audience.

Figure 6.13
The West Lobby in The Cosmopolitan of Las Vegas, USA, 2010, by Rockwell Group's LAB. This immersive, interactive digital experience uses technology to alter, and continually transform, your experience of the interior by blurring the relationship between the digital and the physical realms.

6.13

The use of light and shadow

The West Lobby is just one of a series of spaces that the Rockwell group re-imagined. However, this space, by introducing the majority of guests to the hotel, had to

'deliver a truly larger-than-life, sophisticated, outside the box experience, unlike any other in Las Vegas'[18]

(Core 77 Design Awards, 2011).

This was achieved through the choreographing of an interactive digital interior environment that started from the premise: 'What if no two visits were the same?'[19] (Rockwell, 2014: 302). The space of the West Lobby was characterized by a lack of windows, intersected by eight large, structural columns. Rockwell's LAB aimed to 'dematerialize' these columns by concealing them behind 384 frameless LCD screens and two-way mirrored glass. When the screens were activated, they transformed the interior into a space filled with light and moving imagery, enhanced by reflective floor and ceiling finishes. To achieve this, LAB developed an environmental choreography system known as Spacebrew.

Narrative

This deliberate fusing of the digital and the physical realms has resulted in an immersive interior that transforms instantly. What started as just three digital experiences has now grown to over forty; for Walton, they:

Can manipulate the mood of the space by quickly dialling it up or down. It extends the life of what is exciting and new.[20]

(Tichenor and Walton, 2012)

As Tichenor states, these digital experiences are based upon 'generative software' – so, rather than an endlessly replaying video, you have an environment that constantly changes, offering endless permutations. This, in turn, is linked to motion sensors; when guests enter, self-generating patterns create unique, ever-evolving digital imagery. This becomes a narrative of digital storytelling choreographed onto the surface of the interior setting, flooding a dark space with moving light. This cleverly alludes to the showmanship and razzmatazz that are synonymous with Vegas. As an introduction to the hotel, this example offers a psychological promise of what is yet to come in this weekend away. By introducing the notion of spectacle to the designed interior, this digital interface helps us to rethink the role of surface as a transformative device within any interior mise-en-scène.

Conclusion

This chapter's investigation served as an introduction to light and shadow by exploring their role in informing atmosphere, whilst simultaneously proposing the theory that light as one of the key 'psychological' ingredients of mise-en-scène can potentially taint our perception of interior space. The four suggested headings of natural, artificial, candle, and digital light have simply helped to highlight for the reader the application of these ideas, in line with the chapter focus. So can the consideration of light and shadow substantiate the idea of an interior mise-en-scène?

Both Murnau's *Nosferatu* and The Sam Wanamaker Playhouse use light and shadow evocatively to inform atmosphere. *Nosferatu* clearly illustrates how filmic shadows can be used malevolently to both animate an interior and convey a sense of dread. This type of celluloid image has become ingrained culturally within our collective psyche, and is still exploited cinematically to evoke our childish fear of the dark. Bachelard (1958), as noted in the opening introduction, wrote eloquently of our spatial imagination being informed by both our dreams and our nightmares, and this is clearly seen in this cinematic exploitation of shadows. The use of shadows clearly deserves to become an integral component of any interior mise-en-scène. Their celluloid presence raises interesting questions regarding the interpretation of these ingredients within the context of interior design, whilst suggesting that the ability to understand atmosphere in all its permutations is important.

The Sam Wanamaker Playhouse uses candlelight to inform the staging of performances via the dramatic possibilities of light and shadow, additionally, its employment directly contributes to the ambience of a re-imagined Jacobean interior. The use of candlelight psychologically enhances the spirit of the age. Critically, light and its accompanying shadows are being used evocatively to help sustain the notion of a past time, reinforced by architectural period detail and construction methods. Candlelight obviously carries connotations of a bygone era so it becomes significant as a discernible marker, an essential visual clue that helps to enhance this period scene. Both precedents clearly suggest that shadows are as important as light to the atmosphere of an interior, a realization often overlooked in the development of a lighting scheme.

In contrast, Holl, Eliasson and Rockwell Group's LAB harness the transformative qualities of light. Eliasson's 'phenomena-producers' set out to simulate an extraordinary, artificially lit, light landscape that toys psychologically with our perception of reality. It invites its audience to rethink their expectations of the stereotypical museum setting. The sun's other-worldly light ambience seduces its audience into various attitudes – attitudes more commonly found on a sunny summer beach or in a public park. Interestingly, Eliasson acknowledges the social dimension of his work as an integral ingredient of atmosphere. In other words, people are fundamental to the contrived sense of spectacle. By highlighting the impact that artificial lighting can have upon our impression of an interior, this example also illustrates what can be achieved atmospherically through the use of a very restricted lighting palette.

Holl concentrates upon the transformative effect of natural light magically imbued by hidden colour. This is harnessed as ever-changing phenomena, affected by the rising and setting of the sun, by changing qualities of light, even by the day's weather, and this continually enriches the audience's or user's impression of the interior. Tanizaki's writings (1933), favouring an immaterial or sensory appreciation of atmosphere, clearly resonate.

Temporal or diurnal change raises an interesting proposition regarding the potentially fickle nature of natural lighting. This encourages the design student to consider the unpredictable qualities of atmosphere, as its consideration at an earlier stage clearly enriches space atmospherically.

Finally, Rockwell Group's LAB utilize digital light to transform a dark, subterranean interior into a public space of interactive drama within the West Lobby of The Cosmopolitan. This animated backdrop acknowledges the man-made spectacle of Vegas and its famous strip by creating an encounter that hopes to be in stark contrast to the everyday. It clearly acts as an important introduction to the inner world of the hotel and its brand values, of being subsumed into another realm through its conscious mimicry of Vegas showmanship. This suggests that the splicing of the digital with the physical is a potentially rich area within the context of this book. Its consideration as a technologically driven kinetic 'decorative' layer expands the notion of what can be utilized to alter the surface of interior space. These concluding chapter case studies aim to illustrate the power of light and shadow atmospherically, as well as reinforcing their role as an integral ingredient of any interior mise-en-scène.

FURTHER READING – EXPLORING LIGHT AND SHADOW

This chapter concludes with a suggestion of further reading, an expansion of some of the topics recently introduced. This cinematic reappraisal of interior space aims to recognize the value of shadows alongside the impact of light. It considers light as a constantly changing phenomenon that can be harnessed or manufactured, potentially adding a rich layer of spectacle and showmanship to any interior space.

In Praise of Shadows, written by Japanese novelist Jun'ichiro Tanizaki, was originally published in 1933 although the English translation did not appear until 1977. This seminal book explores Japanese aesthetics through a comparative evaluation of an Eastern versus a Western appreciation of beauty. It is a beautifully written tract that resonates with a sensory appreciation of space, rendered through its description of light and shadow.

Steven Holl: Colour Light Time (2012), co-authored by Jordi Safont-Tria, Sanford Kwinter and Steven Holl, sets out, through three essays, their thoughts on the poetic potential of these phenomena. For them, light and colour enhance the built environment as seen through the ever-changing concept of time.

The Haunted Screen: Expressionism in the German Cinema (1969), by author Lotte H. Eisner, explores the impact of German expressionism on cinematic imagery and traces the legacy of this movement through the vocabulary of film.

7 Colour

A Technicolor© inner world

Color [*sic*] aesthetics may be approached from these three directions: Impression (visually), Expression (emotionally), Construction (symbolically).[1]

(Itten, 1970: 13)

Figure 7.1
Painting fifteen miles of scenery for London pantomime, 1932.
Any analysis of interior atmosphere has to consider the role of colour, whilst an interior mise-en-scène offers the opportunity to examine colour's psychological aspect or tendencies.

Introducing colour

It can come as no great surprise to the reader of this chapter that the application of colour to interior space can quickly and radically transform interior atmosphere. With this in mind, colour theory has become a burgeoning area of investigation for the budding psychologist, colour theorist or designer. Many of the colour theories developed during the eighteenth, nineteenth and twentieth century explore the use of the 'colour wheel' as a system for organizing, categorizing and, ultimately, choosing a colour palette. The work of Johannes Itten and Johann Wolfgang von Goethe is particularly pertinent here; their ideas with regard to colour will be explored in due course.

Colour theory encompasses both the physical and psychological properties of colour. Within interiors, colour can physically communicate how space is organized by highlighting spatial zones and areas of circulation; colour through this process can clearly be used pragmatically as a visual marker. But colour can also radically alter mood and be central to challenging our perception of a given space – this introduces colour psychology into the realm of interior design. The extensive writings of colour theorist Faber Birren (1900–88) elucidate his stance on colour via an understanding of 'physiological and psychological reactions'[2] (1969: 399). This suggests that colour can be viewed as one of the key psychological ingredients of any interior mise-en-scène; the focus for this chapter relates to this topic:

CHAPTER FOCUS

- An introduction to the role of 'colour, graphics and pattern' within interior design.
- An exploration of colour strategies and their role in organizing space and enhancing interior atmosphere.
- An analysis of the psychological 'tendencies' of colour and their contribution towards an interior mise-en-scène.

Colour and atmosphere

Within the interior, colour can be considered as more than just flat blocks or swathes painted onto any available surface. Colour can be introduced through the use of pattern, graphics, materials and lighting. Previous chapters have already explored the role of lighting within interior space and assessed materials through the concept of an interior setting or decorative backdrop. This chapter will concentrate upon strategies common to the application of colour within interior space that have not previously been discussed, although there will be by necessity some overlap. To help engender a quick overview for the reader, colour will be loosely grouped into three categories, each of which will be

discussed in the summary and through the more detailed precedents to follow. These three groupings are:

1. Colour;
2. Colour via pattern;
3. Colour via graphics.

This chapter does not set out to be an exhaustive compendium of every conceivable colour combination, instead it aims to reveal through analysis the strategies and thinking behind certain colour choices within a realized interior scheme.

Colour

All colour studies build upon, and owe a debt to, the discoveries and writings of two practitioners: the physicist Sir Isaac Newton (1642–1727) and the theorist Johann Wolfgang von Goethe (1749–1832). Newton's scientific study of colour published in 1704 revealed colour as a property of light, centred on the refraction of light through a prism to reveal the spectrum of the rainbow. Goethe's writings originally published in 1810 as the *Theory of Colours* famously criticized Newton's scientific study of colour phenomena. Instead, Goethe proffered a highly personal reading organized by chromatic phenomena that he termed the physiological, the physical and the chemical, whilst also connecting emotion to colour through their 'moral' associations. The writings of Newton and Goethe crystallized debate and helped to develop two polarized schools of thought. All resultant colour theories seem to occupy either a rational or an emotional stance.

The colour wheel (prevalent within colour theory) emerged as a logical means for developing colour combinations and both Newton and Goethe used this device. Many other systems of colour have grown from these early studies, notably Albert H. Munsell's (1858–1918) numerical categorization of colour known as the Munsell Colour System. This developed through an analysis of hue (pure colour), value (colours that progress from lightness to darkness) and chroma (colour saturation). Johannes Itten (1888–1967) was famously the colour master at the Bauhaus, important because of its newly emergent design curriculum in the early twentieth century. His teachings, essentially his life's work, are published in *The Art of Colour* (1961) and the abridged version *The Elements of Colours* (1970). Both books concentrated upon the development of a twelve-part colour wheel composed of primary, secondary and tertiary, or intermediate, colours that were used to explore his famous seven key colour contrasts.

An understanding of the colour wheel leads to a mastery of colour concerned with complementary and analogous, as well as warm and cool, colour combinations. Complementary colours geographically sit directly opposite each other on the colour wheel and are concerned with strong contrasts, whilst analogous colours are about adjacency, or similarity in tone (see Figure 7.2). Warm tones relate to colour hues that suggest a 'sensation of temperature' or illusory heat, with blue–green typically suggesting coolness, whilst red–orange denotes warmth. These colour studies also explore and record the optical impact of certain colour combinations, perhaps

7.2

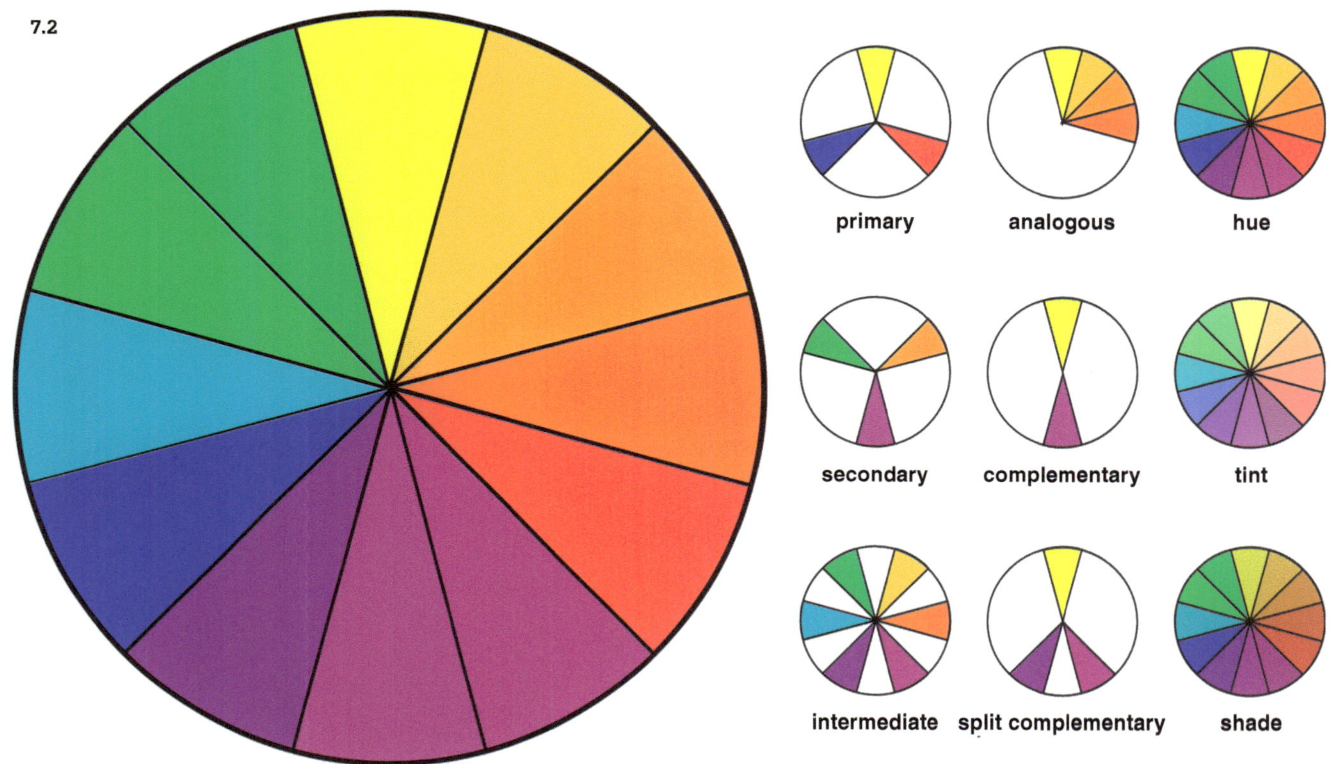

Figure 7.2
The colour wheel.
A simplified set of colour wheels illustrates immediately to the right of the large colour wheel – 'primary colours' (the three colours that cannot be created by the mixing of other colours), 'secondary colours' (formed by mixing two primary colours together), and 'tertiary' or 'intermediate colours' (formed by blending adjacent primary and secondary colours together).

most famously realized in the paintings of Josef Albers (a former student turned master of the Bauhaus), regarding our perceptual reading of distance, space and scale relative to the colour used. The following descriptions aim to illustrate these different approaches to colour.

'The Theme Rooms' by Dutch exhibition designers TRAAST + GRUSON utilized one intense shade of colour to evoke an optical effect at the Centraal Museum. This colour choice aimed to contrast the cool blue of the surroundings against the dark tones of the seventeenth-century oil paintings. Perceptually this colour experiment, with its background of brightly painted skin, aimed to imply new ways of seeing and appreciating the paintings. The canvases within this setting became transformed into 'luminous portals'[3] (Ferrill, 2001: 64). By utilizing a contrasting complementary colour, this realized scheme highlights how colour choice can influence our perception spatially.

Colour was also important to the American artist Andy Warhol (1928–87), perennially popular long after his death because of his iconic pop-art images. He inhabited an equally mythical setting – that of the 'Factory'. Originally sited in a disused warehouse on East 47th Street, New York, the Factory became the location for Warhol where, Svengali-like, he held court, surrounded by the 'Warhol Superstars', a coterie of misfits, artists and hangers-on. The Factory became synonymous with this decadent underground scene as its interior became encased in a skin of silver foil, silver spray-paint and mirrored reflective surfaces. Central to this decorative excess was Warhol's self-proclaimed interior decorator Billy Name. Warhol in his autobiography explains the significance of the colour choice, and this raises interesting questions regarding colour's symbolic or cultural associations:

Silver was the future, it was spacy [*sic*] – the astronauts wore silver suits – Shepherd, Grissom, and Glenn had already been up in them, and their equipment was silver too. And silver was also the past – the Silver Screen – Hollywood actresses photographed in silver sets. And maybe more than anything, silver was narcissism – mirrors were backed with silver.[4]

(Warhol and Hackett, [1981] 1996: 64–5)

Both Itten and Panton expand upon this cultural understanding of colour in their writings: essentially, how colour can borrow meaning and symbolism from historical, ritual or, as highlighted by Warhol, certain cultural situations.

7.3

Figure 7.3
The Theme Rooms, Centraal Museum, Utrecht, Netherlands, 2000, by TRAAST + GRUSON (now credited to ProArtsDesign and Eword Traast).
Colour – a strongly contrasting complementary colour, in this instance blue, employs a dominant colour field to great effect as a foil to the darker tones found in this collection of seventeenth-century paintings.

Colour via pattern

Colour can also be introduced through pattern, which is created through repeated pictorial elements, usually available in a whole series of variable colour options. Aesthetically, pattern can be floral, striped, dotted or swirled, dramatic or subtle, textured or flocked, feature figures, scenes or other recurring motifs. Motif remains central to pattern as it is largely concerned with repetition. Pattern can help to homogenize an interior through its extensive usage within an interior scheme; it can evoke a certain character or period; it can even be used to distort or disorientate. The following descriptions aim to illustrate some striking approaches to the introduction of colour through pattern by highlighting its starring role with regard to interior atmosphere.

The Scottish artist Jim Lambie is perhaps best known for his use of stripes and the creation of immersive patterned environments. Developed through the use of everyday vinyl tape, he explores the wholesale application of pattern. Applied to just one surface (usually the floor), his labour-intensive, patterned signature spaces, known collectively as 'Zobop', overload the senses visually as they disorientate and mesmerize in equal measure. A simple process tracks the outlines of the host space moving ever inwards, until the floor plane is filled with pattern that contributes towards an optically site-specific installation. This approach instantly transforms the audience's impression of an interior space, suggesting that considerations of scale are integral to the impact of colour.

Figure 7.4 'Zobop', Biennale of Sydney, Museum of Contemporary Art, Australia, 2014 by artist Jim Lambie.
Colour as pattern – Lambie's 'Zobop' floor installations dominate space hierarchically by introducing a kaleidoscopic, visually disorientating sense of colour through pattern.

In contrast, the period 1870–1955 saw the rise of the society or 'lady' decorator[5] (Lewis, 2010) and they were viewed as individuals who understood taste, who were educated, worldly women who could deliver the right 'look' for their wealthy, high-society clientele. Dorothy Draper became known for her 'modern baroque' style. This signature aesthetic was known for its bold use of colour and pattern, over-scaled bespoke plaster ornamentation, vivid flora prints, bold stripes rendered in intense candy shades, all offset by chequered black-and-white floors. This aesthetic approach, essentially a 'modified Victorian style'[6] (Varney, 1988: 240), was implemented in one of her most famous commissions, the refurbishment of the historic Greenbrier Hotel and its sprawling estate in White Sulphur Springs, West Virginia. This example highlights how a decorator with an established style can utilize colour and pattern combinations to win commissions and successfully 'draperize' an interior.

Colour via graphics

The final category in this chapter explores the application of graphics and their role in adding colour to interior space. In its simplest form this can be applied directly to a room as a painted bespoke surface by an artist or decorator. Alternatively, it can be introduced through images imprinted onto wallpaper or even projected visuals. This forms a pictorial backdrop, a talking point, a piece of scenery around which a space can be organized. These graphics can become large-scale room-sized scenographic incidents that rethink dramatically the more traditional role of the decorative skin; alternatively, they can be rescaled becoming a discrete interplay of smaller recurring motifs, an approach illustrated by the following description.

7.5

7.6

Figures 7.5 and 7.6
The Greenbrier Hotel, White Sulphur Springs, USA, 1948, by Dorothy Draper & Company, Inc.
Colour as pattern – Draper became synonymous with her signature 'modern baroque' style, an approach that regularly introduced vivid colours and flamboyant pattern to interior schemes.

Figures 7.7 and 7.8
Witloof restaurant, Maastricht, Belgium, 2005, by designer Maurice Mentjens.
Colour as pattern and graphics – Mentjens introduces colour through meaningful pattern and graphics in the staging of individual interior vignettes that reference both the cuisine of the country and its regional character.

7.7

7.8

Witloof restaurant, located in Maastricht by Dutch designer Maurice Mentjens, uses colour through pattern and graphics to zone a series of different dining experiences. The restaurant celebrates Belgian cuisine, so the diner enters a series of carefully orchestrated interior atmospheres that contextually reference this heritage. Mentjens describes how he was inspired by a visit to the country and how he responded by 'combining three interiors that typify Belgian cafes and restaurants'[7] (Mentjens, 2005). Narratively, the spaces encountered atmospherically evoke through their use of materials and pattern a log cabin, a metropolitan chip shop, and a typical Belgian drawing room lined with green baroque wallpaper. Downstairs, in the ancient medieval cellar, a dining space conceived as an archetypal crypt uses a black Gothic-revival pattern. In 2010 this space became transformed into a seductive dining area adorned with huge Rubenesque graphics of scantily clad Greek and Roman goddesses. This example suggests that colour and pattern, if recognizably stereotypical, can be used evocatively to suggest place as well as to stage a series of distinct interior vignettes.

Examples of interior mise-en-scène, using colour

In any discussion of colour, Faber Birren's extensive work as both a colour consultant and author should be considered. His comments regarding the phenomenon of colour within a man-made environment are pertinent, namely 'the safe course to take, perhaps, is neither to accept nor deny the phenomenal, but to speak of tendencies'[8] (1969: 399). For Birren, any choice of colour was closely aligned with colour phenomenon via empirically established human reaction and responses, an approach that has been quickly ridiculed by the gainsayers and sceptics. But these recurring concerns do raise interesting questions regarding the psychological impact of colour, an area that is, and continues to be, hotly debated.

The five case studies included in this chapter all aim to highlight and discuss how colour, pattern and graphics can be introduced in a meaningful way to interior space. They aim to expose the underlying strategies relating to the psychological impact of colour theory, as well as to the use of colour as a structural system that organizes the physical space of the interior. Examples will be drawn from the usual eclectic mix of artists, designers and film-makers and will encompass healthcare, office refurbishment, art installations, hotel design and cinematic settings. Each precedent will be analysed through the usual headings of context and narrative, whilst special attention is this time given to the use of colour.

Case Study One: Colour – *The Cook, The Thief, His Wife and Her Lover*, director Peter Greenaway

The greens of the kitchen, apart from indicating safety, suggest the color [*sic*] of nature – therefore its healing and embracing, the color [*sic*] of chlorophyll. Green represents the mythological jungle where all the food comes from. Red means violence, carnivorousness, blood – the dining room where the centre of violence happens.[9]

(Greenaway, cited in Siegel, 1990: 76–7)

Context

Released in 1989, British director Peter Greenaway's *The Cook, The Thief, His Wife and Her Lover* divided critical opinion over his decision to explore cinematically several controversial subjects – namely, human corporeality and cannibalism. The film's story, essentially a tale of revenge, centres upon a bullying gangster, the thief (Spica), his long-suffering and abused wife (Georgina), her lover (Michael), and the chef (Richard), the owner of the restaurant. The film famously concludes with Spica being forced to eat the cooked corpse of his wife's lover in an act of allegorical storytelling. Greenaway's work historically sits outside mainstream cinema and is art-house in nature. Influenced by his early studies as a painter and his love of European art history, Greenaway seeks to create an alternative, non-narrative, cinematic vocabulary and structure for his films through symbolism. This case study has been included because of its exemplary use of colour to help establish this cinematic language.

Use of colour

The majority of the story takes place in a fictional restaurant, Le Hollandais, where Spica and his cronies dine nightly, and entertain themselves by terrorizing the restaurant staff and their fellow diners. Greenaway's vision is realized by regular collaborators, cinematographer Sachs Vierny and production designers Ben van Os and Jan Roelfs. The setting for this violent tale is vividly brought to life by Greenaway's use of 'colour-coding'. He famously employs a six-part colour system that allocates colour zonally to a specific room within the restaurant; even the characters' flamboyant costumes change in response to this rule: typically,

'Blue for the car park; green for the kitchen; red for the restaurant; white for the toilet; yellow for the hospital; and a golden hue for the book depository'[10]

(ibid.: 76).

These zones also operate expressively to conjure particular psychological connotations through their associated colour tendencies.

The kitchen becomes a safe zone for the lovers, a place where they can escape Spica and somewhere they are often naked. It becomes a metaphorical Garden of Eden and, as a consequence of this implied meaning, is given an appropriate green hue. The toilet becomes white, linked to heaven, where the lovers first consummate their relationship. Conversely, the sumptuous red restaurant relates to violence, tension and heightened emotions and is dramatically coloured. An oversized painting by the seventeenth-century Dutch artist Frans Hals adds a silent audience of voyeuristic spectators to further intimidate and unsettle in an intricately realized, highly coloured mise-en-scène. Slow, horizontal tracking shots reveal these coloured spaces as a 'painted frieze'[11] (Woods, 1996: 240), a sectional view that helps to establish the interior geography of the set whilst simultaneously revealing scenes overflowing with decorative detail.

Narrative

Greenaway views himself as a painter working in film and is interested in developing alternative visual means for organizing the cinematic frame. Much has already been written of his love of encyclopedic systems of organization – of which, colour is just one. This colour-coding not only defines and characterizes the spaces of the film functionally, but also seeks to suggest psychologically the tendencies these spaces harbour. It is this duality that parallels the design of interiors, as colour can be allocated as a spatial system of organization, as well as aligned with specific spaces because of its psychological overtones.

Figure 7.9
The Cook, The Thief, His Wife and Her Lover, 1989, director **Peter Greenaway.** The use of colour by director Peter Greenaway structures the space of the film territorially whilst these colour zones also operate expressively, conjuring psychological connotations through their associated colour tendencies.

Case Study Two: Colour – Spiegel Publishing Headquarters by Verner Panton

Choosing colours should not be a gamble. It should be a conscious decision. Colours have meaning and function.[12]

(Panton, 1997: Preface)

Context

The Danish designer and architect Verner Panton (1926–98) is remembered as much for his contribution to twentieth-century product and textile design as for his use of colour. Synonymous with the sixties, Panton developed a colour palette via a personalized theory, realized through a series of vividly rendered optical environments and public commissions that included the legendary 'Phantasy Landscape' for 'Visiona 2' (1970). Prior to this, Panton developed a colour strategy for the Spiegel Publishing House in Hamburg, Germany in 1969. This case study has been included because it clearly illustrates Panton's empirically established colour theory.

Use of colour

Panton's ideas concentrated upon the development of holistically derived introverted environments of intense colour, and the Spiegel interior is essentially an exercise in

7.10

'colour-planning'. This unified approach to colour, form, pattern, textiles and lighting was referred to by Panton as a 'milieu'[13] (Epple, 2000: 159). Housed in a mundane building, the space was retrofitted as the company headquarters. Colour was used to zone the interior spatially and as a means by which departments became characterized visually. This homogenized, polychromatic environment also aimed to alter the mood of rooms by considering the impact of colour psychologically.

The Spiegel interior initially consisted of twelve floors that were duly assigned one colour each from a twelve-part colour wheel (Panton's preferred colour system). Colour was further allocated according to its perceived psychological tendencies of warmth or coolness. Green, as a cool tone for Panton, equated to calmness, so it was assigned to the waiting area, whereas red as a warm tone related to communication, so this was assigned to the communal canteen, and to the snack area. Additionally, blue and green as cool tones correlated to increased concentration, so these were used in the offices of the editorial staff[14] (Ott, 2009–10: 110–1).

Narrative

Panton clearly uses colour to build a relationship between the physical applications of colour to space, informed by its psychological tendencies. His book *Notes on Colour* explores these colour tendencies further by assigning psychological properties to nine key colours, typically:

When looking at red, the pulse beats faster, when looking at blue, the pulse beats more slowly ... Red is inspiring and provides an atmosphere for good ideas [whilst] blue is excellent for working with ideas.[15]

(1997: 14)

This approach is clearly influenced by both physiological and culturally established chromatic associations and this suggests that due consideration should be given to the language of colour. Its associations and tendencies beyond a purely aesthetic application should be evaluated within the context of an interior mise-en-scène.

Figures 7.10 and 7.11 **Spiegel Publishing Headquarters, Hamburg, Germany, 1969 by Verner Panton.** Panton's colour planning correlated to the spatial organization of the building whilst he also applied colour theory psychologically, matching warm tones (Figure 7.10 – The Canteen) and cool tones (Figure 7.11 – The Waiting Room) to their most appropriate activity.

Case Study Three: Colour via pattern – 'Dots Obsession' by Yayoi Kusama

In fact, I often suffered episodes of severe neurosis. I would cover a canvas with nets, then continue painting them on the table, on the floor, and finally on my own body. As I repeated this process over and over again, the nets began to expand to infinity. I forgot about myself as they enveloped me, clinging to my arms and legs and clothes and filling the entire room.[16]

(Kusama, [2002] 2011: 20)

**Figure 7.12
'Dots
Obsession',
2009, artist
Yayoi Kusama,
'Walking in my
Mind'
exhibition at
the Hayward
Gallery,
London.** Kusama introduces colour through an all-encompassing pattern, an approach that transforms interior space through 'obliteration' in a highly personal interpretation of her mental illness and its bearing on her perception of space.

Context

The Japanese artist Yayoi Kusama, born in 1929, is perhaps best known for her immersive installations where pattern runs amok, investing interior space with a new character by literally obliterating its previous identity. This all-encompassing use of pattern has resulted in some instantly recognizable interiors, and this case study has been included because of Kusama's extensive use of pattern to inform and characterize space. Throughout her life, Kusama has struggled with mental illness, becoming regularly hospitalized, so that her art has become a form of self-therapy that she refers to as 'Psychomatic Art'[17] (ibid.: 42).

Use of colour

The move from paintings, especially her dotted 'Infinity Net' series, into large-scale habitats allowed this patterned vocabulary, central to her *oeuvre*, to be expressed spatially. These decorated environments have become signature pieces, which since the sixties have been recreated to order internationally. Her 'Dots Obsession' installation from 2009 is typical of this repetitive approach to colour and pattern. By using simple props, in this instance large, amorphous inflatable balloons alongside wall mirrors that partially line the perimeter, everything from the walls, floors, ceiling, through to the inflatables is covered by a recurring motif of red and white polka dots. The mirrors reflect this pattern to create an infinite, artificially spotted ambience.

Narrative

Kusama's autobiography (2002) details an event that helps us to understand, as well as explain, her artistic practice. Her illness manifested itself as hallucinations from a young age, and she describes an episode involving a patterned tablecloth that became imprinted upon her body and the surrounding space, literally 'obliterating' her sense of self[18] (ibid.: 69–70). These hallucinations have led to an obsessive interest in ceaseless, compulsively produced patterns, a narrative that clearly drives her work. Her installations engender a sense of disorientation and confusion (akin to Kusama's delusions) precisely because of their pervasive use of pattern. The introduction of colour through pattern is memorable because it homogenizes interior space and the objects it contains, transforming it through this process. Pattern is used to 'obliterate' its previous identity. This example illustrates how colour can be applied through pattern, pattern that because of its wholesale application dominates visually via a repetitively enhanced interior mise-en-scène.

Case Study Four: Colour via graphics – The Hotel by Jean Nouvel

I'm no magician, but I try to create a space that isn't legible, a space that works as the mental extension of sight. This seductive space, this virtual space of illusion, is based on very precise strategies, strategies that are often diversionary.[19]

(Jean Nouvel, in Baudrillard and Nouvel, [2000] 2002: 06)

Context

The Hotel, located in Lucerne, Switzerland, completed in 2000, was refurbished by French architect Jean Nouvel whose architectural *oeuvre* has, by his own admission, become linked to 'transparency'. This has been achieved through an 'aesthetics of disappearance'[20] (ibid.: 17) that plays with the illusory qualities of surface to dematerialize his buildings. The case study for this boutique hotel has been included in this chapter because the building adheres to these preoccupations, but utilizes colourful graphics to invoke spatial transparency through ambiguity. It achieves this through the application of diversionary tactics relating to Nouvel's 'architectural bag of tricks'[21] (ibid.: 08).

Use of colour

Film stills are up-scaled to the size of a guest room and encase entire ceilings graphically. The scale of implementation invites parallels with scenography as each room becomes a conceptual backdrop to these gargantuan images. Guests lying in bed are completely immersed by these carefully chosen film images (in reality, intimate scenes of lovers and their relationships taken from a role call of

contemporary cinema). The choice of image helps to determine the subsequent colour palette of the rooms as well as its furnishings; cleverly, the dark interior is subservient to the richness and intensity proffered by the ceiling graphics.

7.13

Narrative

The narrative at work here is one of transparency, achieved through 'cinematic voyeurism'[22] (Chen, 2001: 268). Colourful graphics match the scale of the rooms and self-consciously invite the gaze of passers-by on the street outside, exposing the inner life of the hotel. This is the architectural equivalent of looking into the lit rooms of houses at night before the curtains are drawn. Other concepts of voyeurism run through the hotel, most notably in the basement restaurant where mirrors are used to reflect the street scenes above to the diners below. The inherently private becomes a matter of public consumption as the guest rooms become re-imagined as a tableau of pictorial canvases that operate holistically, to become an architecturally scaled billboard. The graphics are successful because of their colour, number, scale and placement, achieving interior transparency through a playful architectural depth of field concerned with exposure. These interior scenes are brought sharply into focus once the lights come on and night coalesces, cleverly creating a strong brand and street presence for this hotel. Graphics remain central to this revelatory process and this highlights their importance within the concept of an interior mise-en-scène.

7.14

Figures 7.13 and 7.14
The Hotel, Lucerne, Switzerland, 2000, by Jean Nouvel.
Nouvel plays with the concept of 'cinematic voyeurism' via scenic backdrops. Architecturally scaled graphics encase the entire ceilings of the hotel's bedrooms to create pictorial incidents for both guests and spectators on the street outside.

Case Study Five: Colour – Wards 23 and 29, Bradford Royal Infirmary

This is a ground-breaking initiative for the trust and it is already making a huge difference by quickly and clearly illustrating how relatively small changes to the hospital environment can reduce anxiety, accidents and incidents of challenging behaviour.[23]

(Dawn Parkes, Head of Nursing, cited in *Building Better Healthcare*, 2012)

Context

Within the healthcare sector a well-designed environment is increasingly being viewed as beneficial to both patients and staff alike. With this in mind, this case study chronicles the refurbishment of Wards 23 and 29 at Bradford Royal Infirmary (part of the Bradford Teaching Hospitals NHS Foundation Trust), important because of its exemplary use of colour to aid patients' well-being and enhance their spatial awareness during a hospital stay. Located in West Yorkshire, England, both wards cater for elderly patients, many evidencing signs of dementia. The refurbishment was led by a multidisciplinary team composed of medical practitioners and specialists in the care of patients of this type and was completed in 2012. Dementia is a debilitating, progressive disease that affects memory, cognitive abilities and social interaction as you grow older. Any hospital stay can be an unsettling experience, but this is especially true for dementia patients who struggle to adapt to unfamiliar surroundings.

Use of colour

The role of colour within this clinical setting is used to transform interior atmosphere as well as to help vulnerable patients to navigate the space.

Figures 7.15 and 7.16 Wards 23 and 29, Bradford Royal Infirmary, Bradford, England, 2012. An award-winning healthcare refurbishment uses incidents of colour, supported by props, to aid orientation and memory for its vulnerable patients.

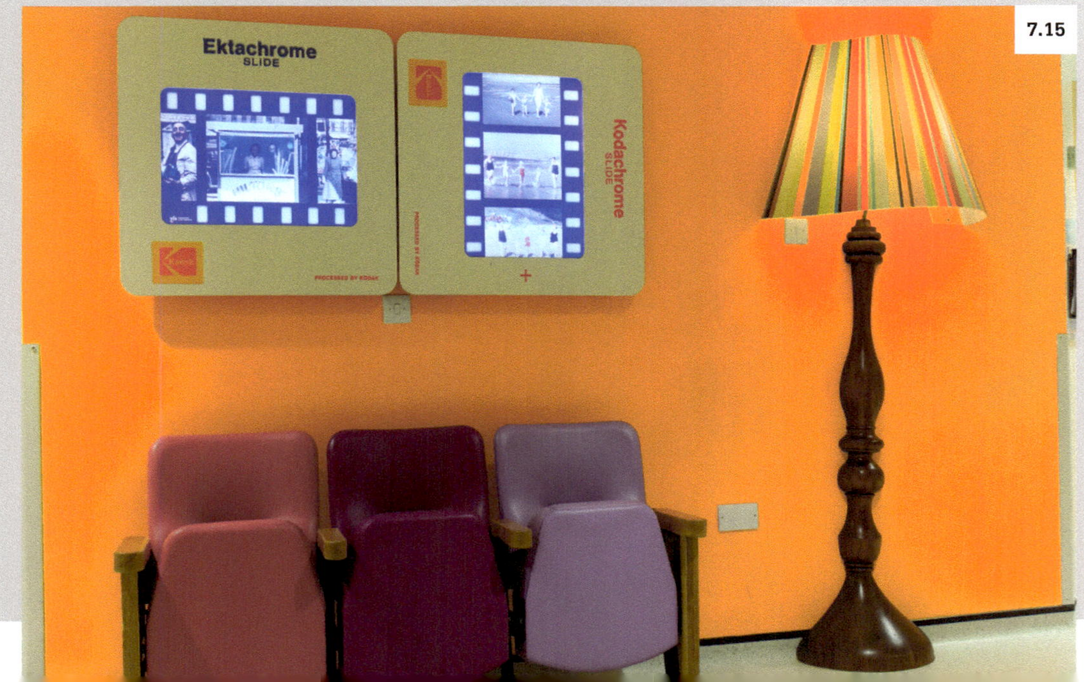

The typically repetitive, bland corridors, unfortunately common to many healthcare environments, house colourful landmarks that aid orientation. Oversized residential props, such as standard lamps with striped shades, are fixed to brightly coloured walls, whilst immediately adjacent is equally vibrant cinema-style seating. Above this, illuminated wall-mounted boxes display ever-changing archive images of local scenes and events. This is clearly a sensitive attempt to prompt patients' memories and encourage discussion and conversation, which is further enhanced by bedside memory boxes and reminiscence tables.

The choice of colours in this instance – tones of orange, purple, lilac and raspberry – create an incident of colour, a punctuation mark within a bland environment that helps to act as a memory aid to its community of patients. This colour-coding is extended so that patients can easily find their way back to their beds or from other facilities. Sample colour boards had been displayed in both wards so that patients, visitors and staff could be integral to the selection of the final colour palette.

Narrative

The scheme won a national healthcare design award in 2012, but perhaps more importantly it was part of a larger government initiative to promote simple, cost-effective design alterations to clinical environments that would make them more dementia-friendly. The design principles of legibility, orientation, way-finding, familiarity and meaningful activity[24] (Stanley, 2013: 70) were seen as central to many of the improvements made. The development of a colourful interior mise-en-scène clearly resonates with the first three of these design principles, and has been linked to increased orientation, reduced patient agitation and incidents of challenging behaviour[25] (ibid.: 81–5, 91). This example illustrates the important role that colour can take in the well-being of the patient and highlights the consideration that should be given to meaningful colour strategies as an integral component of any healthcare scheme.

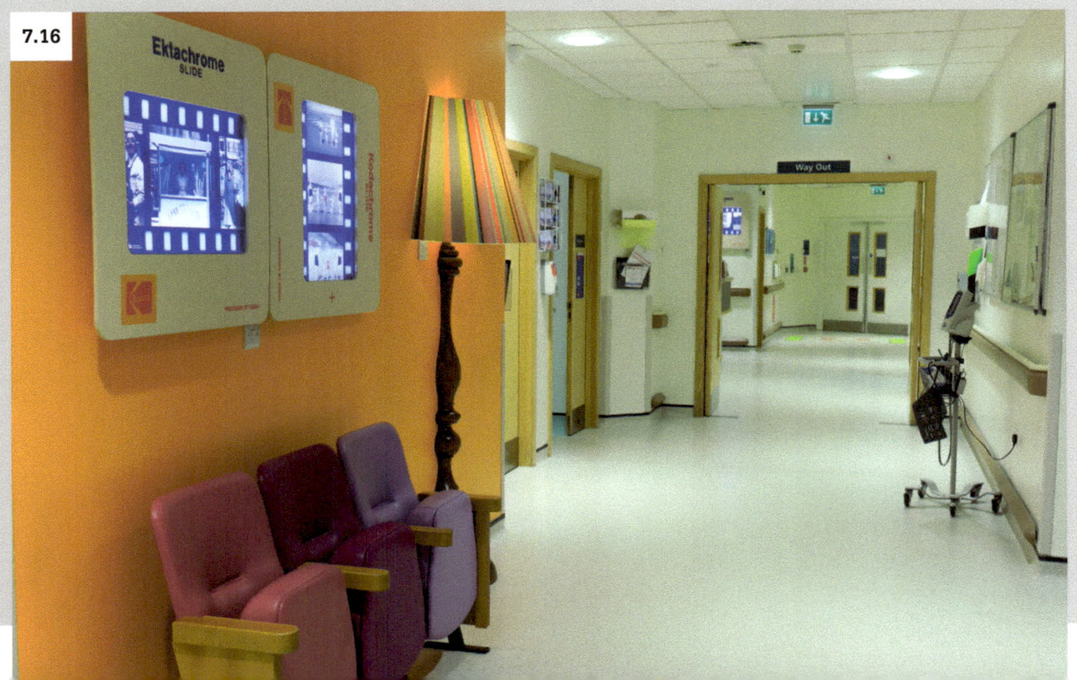

7.16

Conclusion

This chapter set out to explore the role of colour strategically, whilst simultaneously evaluating its inclusion as a core ingredient of any interior mise-en-scène. The three headings relating to colour, pattern, and graphics initially helped to circumscribe interiors that share a common approach. Of especial interest is the role that colour assumed, or was thought to assume, physically (through its spatial application and organization), and psychologically (through its atmosphere). By drawing upon the focus outlined at the beginning of this chapter, it is clear that this serves as an introduction to the role of colour, graphics and pattern within interior design. The exploration of colour strategies and their role in organizing space and enhancing interior atmosphere was integral to this. The following observations have been made relating to the five main case studies.

Greenaway clearly uses colour-coding to organize visually the space of the film. Colour is used territorially to quickly establish a relationship to a particular 'room' within the screenplay. Framing, composition and colour are central to the visual legibility of each scene, and to the narrative as a whole. In a similar manner, the colourful world of Panton encapsulates an approach that uses colour to literally 'construct' space holistically. For Panton, 'colour-planning' became a system for organizing space according to its function and identity. Comparably, the refurbished wards at Bradford Royal Infirmary utilize colour to orientate patients, a form of colourful way-finding within a larger healthcare environment. Of the three examples discussed, it is abundantly clear that they share a common approach to colour relating to increased legibility. This use of colour necessitates a rethinking from colour as a purely decorative device, to one that articulates and legitimates space for the user and its audience through difference.

In parallel with these observations, this chapter also sets out to consider the psychological tendencies of colour. Greenaway's territorial organization of colour is supplemented by symbolic colour tendencies that, for him, invoke certain universal colour associations. This consciously cinematic approach to staging surely resonates with the theoretical stance of an interior mise-en-scène as outlined in this book, and raises interesting questions regarding a prevalent language of colour. Panton echoes Greenaway by matching colour tendencies to usage, mapping their psychological and physiological triggers to certain everyday work situations. The use of colour within healthcare, in this instance, also operates psychologically as an aid to calm patients by making their setting instantly recognizable, even familiar. These precedents through their use of colour clearly parallel the colour theories of Goethe and Itten via their emotive colour associations. Birren highlights two key conclusions with regard to colour that relate to what he terms 'centrifugal' and 'centripetal' action[26] ([1969] 1988: 31). The former refers to a greater awareness of your environment, where high levels of illumination and the use of warm colours suggest increased alertness and interaction. In contrast, the latter, with its use of cooler tones and lower light levels, is more introverted, and hence more conducive to concentrated visual and mental tasks. This creates some strategically useful points of reference for any design student relating to the application of colour to interior space.

In contrast to the three case studies discussed so far, both Kusama and Nouvel use colour differently, introducing it instead through pattern or graphics. Kusama's pervasive use of pattern alters spatial reality through the simple device of decoration. As a direct consequence of pattern, stereotypical rectilinear interior spaces are transformed through a process of metamorphosis. This approach is also utilized by Nouvel as his refurbished hotel interior introduces colour through architecturally conceived graphics. These graphics operate as scenographic devices, essentially a hierarchical backdrop that transforms the interior into a habitable set. Conceptually, this inverts the traditional threshold divisions of inside and outside, public to private, viewer to viewed, and hotel to city.

Pattern and graphics in this instance are transformative, suggesting that their judicious use can significantly impact upon our understanding and perception of space. The intention is that these concluding case studies should all clearly illustrate the impact that colour can have on interior space. Its pervasive influence can be seen through its wholesale application as an aid to spatial legibility, whilst colour tendencies consistently remain one of the more commonly found strategies for implementing a colour system. Colour clearly plays a pivotal role in informing atmosphere compositionally, aesthetically and psychologically, and this can only reinforce its inclusion as a key ingredient of any interior mise-en-scène. As a final comment, it is worth reminding the reader that whilst, for expediency, the ingredients of an interior mise-en-scène have been introduced separately, it is their relationship and their endless combinations that will help to build an intense atmosphere.

FURTHER READING – EXPLORING COLOUR

Through recognition of the inherent duality of colour, any interested party quickly realizes that it can be used to reinforce spatial territories, whilst acknowledgement of its psychological impact on any potential user proffers another avenue of application. Physiological responses to colour have helped to form the basis of current colour psychology, whilst additionally the optical impact spatially of certain colour combinations and contrasts has been highlighted. The suggested books below simply aim to extend these findings through the opportunity of further reading.

Theory of Colours, by Johann Wolfgang von Goethe, originally published in 1810, sets out Goethe's highly personal theory of colour phenomena as a series of subjective experiences. This book still has value, although his critique of Newton's work, with the measure of hindsight, appears rather misguided. Its extensively catalogued observations of colour (see Part I) as well as an early interpretation of colour association through cultural meaning (see Part VI) are worth referencing.

The Elements of Colour (1970), by Bauhaus master Johannes Itten, captures his influential theory of colour through this abridged version of the earlier *The Art of Colour* (1961). This book succinctly establishes his twelve-part colour wheel and the accompanying 'seven key colour contrasts'.

Light, Colour and Environment, by colour author and theorist Faber Birren, originally published in 1969, with a second revised edition dating from 1988, utilizes a series of empirical case studies to underline the impact that light and colour have through their physiological and psychological responses. Birren concludes this book with a series of useful recommendations that explore colour 'tendencies' as applicable to certain interior genres and user groups within the built environment.

Endnotes

Chapter One: Creating interior atmosphere: an introduction

1 Zumthor, P. ([2006] 2015), *Atmospheres: Architectural Environments, Surrounding Objects,* trans. I. Galbraith, reprint, Basel: Birkhauser.

2 Martin, A. (2014), *Mise En Scène and Film Style, From Classical Hollywood to New Media Art,* Basingstoke: Palgrave Macmillan.

3 IFI World (n.d.), 'Definition of a Professional Interior Designer/Architect', *IFI World.* Available online: http://www.ifiworld.org/#Definition_of_an_IA/D (accessed 30 March 2016).

4 Barsacq, L. ([1970] 1976), *Caligari's Cabinet and other Grand Illusions: A History of Film Design,* E. Stein (ed.), trans. M. Bullock, Boston: New York Graphic Society.

5 Oxford Dictionaries (n.d.), 'Atmosphere', *Oxford Dictionaries.* Available online: http://www.oxforddictionaries.com/definition/english/atmosphere (accessed 2 July 2014).

6 Benjamin, W. ([1982] 2002), *The Arcades Project,* trans. H. Eiland and K. McLaughlin, paperback edition, Cambridge, Massachusetts and England: The Belknap Press of Harvard University Press.

7 Ibid.

8 Tanizaki, J. ([1933] 1977), *In Praise of Shadows,* trans. T. J. Harper and E. G. Seidensticker, 8th reprint, Stony Creek: Leete's Island Books Inc.

9 Ibid.

10 Ibid.

11 Pallasmaa, J. (1996), *The Eyes of the Skin: Architecture and the Senses,* London: Academy Editions.

12 Serrres, M. (2008), 'The Five Senses: Boxes', in L. Weinthal (ed.), (2011), *Towards a New Interior: An Anthology of Interior Design Theory,* 267–70, New York: Princeton Architectural Press.

13 Zumthor, *Atmospheres: Architectural Environments, Surrounding Objects,* 19.

14 Bachelard, G. ([1958] 1992), *The Poetics of Space,* trans. M. Jolas, Boston: Beacon Press.

15 Böhme, G. (2013), 'The Art of the Stage Set as a Paradigm for an Aesthetics of Atmosphere', *Ambiances: International Journal of Sensory Environment, Architecture and Urban Space.* Available online: http://ambiances.revues.org/315 (accessed 15 July 2015).

16 Ibid.

17 Griffero, T. ([2010] 2014), [e-book] *Atmospheres: Aesthetics of Emotional Spaces,* trans. S. De Sanctis, London and Farnham: Routledge. Available online: http://site.ebrary.com/lib/falmouth/reader.action?docID=10861723&ppg=4 (accessed 5 February 2016).

18 Pallasmaa, J. (2005), *Encounters: Architectural Essays.* P. Mackeith (ed.), Eng. trans. Diana C. Tullberg and Michael Wynne-Ellis, Helsinki: Rakennustieto Publishing.

Chapter Two: What's in a room? The principles of mise-en-scène

1 Gibbs, J. (2002), *Mise-En-Scène: Film Style and Interpretation.* London: Wallflower Press.

2 Bordwell, D. and Thompson, K. ([1979] 2001), *Film Art: An introduction.* 6th edn, York: McGraw-Hill Higher Education.

3 Gibbs, *Mise-En-Scène: Film Style and Interpretation,* 06–26.

4 Bordwell and Thompson, *Film Art: An introduction,* 158–74.

5 Martin, *Mise En Scène and Film Style, From Classical Hollywood to New Media Art,* 16.

6 Ettedgui, P. (1999), *Production Design & Art Direction,* Crans-Près-Céligny: RotoVision.

7 Schaal, H. D. (2000), 'Spaces of the Psyche in German Expressionist Film', in B. Fear (ed.), *A.D. Architecture + Film II*, 70 (1): 12–15.

8 Pallasmaa, J. (2007), *The Architecture of Image: Existential Space in Cinema,* trans. M. Wynne-Ellis, 2nd edn, Helsinski: Rakennustieto Publishing.

9 Cairns, G. (2013), [e-book] *Architecture of the Screen: Essays in Cinematographic Space,* Bristol and Chicago: Intellect Ltd. Available online: http://site.ebrary.com/lib/falmouth/reader.action?docID=10825865 (accessed 11 July 2016).

10 Martin, *Mise En Scène and Film Style, From Classical Hollywood to New Media Art,* 19–20.

11 Lobrutto, V. (2002), *The Filmmaker's Guide to Production Design,* New York: All Worth Press.

12 Bordwell, D. (2015), 'Wes Anderson takes the 4:3 Challenge', in M. Zoller Seitz, *The Wes Anderson Collection: The Grand Budapest Hotel,* 237–49, New York: Abrams.

13 Boone, S. (2015), 'A Grand Stage: The Production Design of the Grand Budapest Hotel', in M. Zoller Seitz, *The Wes Anderson Collection: The Grand Budapest Hotel*, 143–7, New York: Abrams.

14 Brownlow, K. (1996), *David Lean: A Biography,* New York: Wyatt Book for St. Martins Press.

15 Barsacq, *Caligari's Cabinet and other Grand Illusions: A History of Film Design,* 125.

16 Shakespeare, W. ([1599–1600] 1963), *As You Like It*, A. Gilman (ed.), New York: Signet Classic.

17 Rugoff, R. (2010), 'The New Décor', in R. Rugoff, H. Foster, M. Kuo, C. Lange and S. Sherwin, *The New Décor,* 11–21, London: Hayward Publishing.

18 Colomina, B. ([1994] 1996), *Privacy and Publicity: Modern Architecture as Mass Media.* 1st paperback edn, Cambridge: MIT Press.

19 Foucault, M. ([1975] 1991), *Discipline and Punish: The Birth of the Prison,* trans. A. Sheridan, Middlesex: Penguin Books.

20 Ibid.

21 Gamard, E. B, (2000), *Kurt Schwitters' Merzbau: The Cathedral of Erotic Misery,* New York: Princeton Architectural Press.

22 Betsky, A. (2003), 'Display Engineers', in L. Weinthal (ed.), (2011), *Toward a New Interior: An Anthology of Interior Design Theory,* 559–73, New York: Princeton Architectural Press.

23 Böhme, 'The Art of the Stage Set as a Paradigm for an Aesthetics of Atmosphere'.

Chapter Three: The interior setting: the backdrop or 'skin' of the space

1 Böhme, 'The Art of the Stage Set as a Paradigm for an Aesthetics of Atmosphere'.

2 Metalworks/Surface Architects (2007), *Architects' Journal,* 29 March, 225 (12): 60–71.

3 Ciment, M. and Niogret, H. (1991), 'Regards to Barton Fink', trans. R. Barton Palmer, in R. Barton Palmer (2004), *Joel and Ethan Coen*, 172–92, Urbana and Chicago: University of Illinois Press.

4 Ibid.

5 Guidi, A. C. (1998), [pdf] 'The invisible materiality of air', *Ingesidee.* Available online: http://ingesidee.de/dateien/dokumente/de/hans_hemmert_the_invisible_materiality_of_air_anna_cestelli_guidi_cgac_centro_galego_de_arte_contemporanea_santiago_de_compostella_spain_1998.pdf (accessed 12 July 2015).

6 Denari, N. M. (2002), 'L.A. Eyeworks' *Neil Denari-NMDA.* Available online: http://projects.denari.co/L-A-EYEWORKS-2002 (accessed 7 December 2016).

7 Barsacq, *Caligari's Cabinet and other Grand Illusions: A History of Film Design,* 25.

8 Robinson, D. ([1997] 1999), *Das Cabinet Des Dr. Caligari,* London: BFI Publishing.

9 Sennett, R. S. (1994), *Setting the Scene: The Great Hollywood Art Directors,* New York: Harry N. Abrams Inc.

10 Lee, K. (2011), *Rough Luxe Design: The New Love of the Old,* New York City: Farameh Media LLC.

11 Ibid.

12 Nieswand, N. (2010), 'What Lies Beneath'. *Grand Designs,* May, (75): 92–5.

13 Ibid.

14 Walpole, H. ([1784] 2015), *A Description of the Villa at Strawberry Hill,* facsimile, with an

introduction by S. Clarke and a foreword by M. Snodin, London: Pallas Athene Ltd.

15 Snodin, M. (ed.) (2009), *Horace Walpole's Strawberry Hill,* The Lewis Walpole Library, Yale University, Yale Centre for British Art, Victoria and Albert Museum, New Haven and London: Yale University Press.

16 Snodin, M. (n.d.), [video] *Introducing Strawberry Hill.* Available online: http://www.strawberryhillhouse.org.uk/video1.php (accessed 20 June 2015).

17 Rajagopal, A. (2013), 'The Creative Process: Spatial Conversations – Petra Blaisse', *Metropolis,* 1 March. Available online: http://www.metropolismag.com/March-2013/The-Creative-Process-Spatial-Conversations-Petra-Blaisse/ (accessed 3 June 2015).

18 Blomberg, K., Waldsee, H. A. and GRAFT (eds), (2011), *Distinct Ambiguity: GRAFT.* Eng. trans. of preface, V. Ellerbeck, Berlin: Gestalten.

19 Ibid.

20 Ibid.

21 Ibid.

Chapter Four: What is an interior 'prop'? Accessories, furniture, fixtures and equipment

1 Benjamin, *The Arcades Project,* 218.

2 Groskop, V. (2012), 'How to make a Haunted House', *The Guardian,* 5 February. Available online: https://www.theguardian.com/film/2012/feb/05/woman-in-black-special-effects (accessed 25 July 2016).

3 Swanson, C. (2010), 'Comfort Me with Flanges', *New York Magazine,* 10 October. Available online: http://nymag.com/arts/art/features/68825/ (accessed 9 July 2015).

4 Alesch, S. and Standefer, R. (2012), *Roman and Williams Buildings and Interiors: Things We Made, Part One,* New York: Rizzoli.

5 Ibid.

6 Hughes, R. (1971), 'The Décor of Tomorrow's Hell', in S. Y. McDougal (ed.), (2003), *Stanley Kubrick's A Clockwork Orange,* 131–3, Cambridge: Cambridge University Press.

7 Burgess, A. ([1962] 1982), *A Clockwork Orange,* Middlesex, New York, Victoria, Ontario and Auckland: Penguin Books.

8 Webster, P. (2011), *Love and Death in Kubrick: A Critical Study of the films from Lolita through Eyes Wide Shut,* Jefferson: McFarland & Company Inc.

9 Landy, M. (2001), *Break Down: Michael Landy,* G. van Noord (ed.), London: Artangel.

10 Ibid.

11 Jencks, C. (2010), 'The Architecture of Hope', in C. Jencks and E. Heathcote, *The Architecture of Hope: Maggie's Cancer Caring Centres*, 08-43. London: Frances Lincoln Ltd.

12 Jencks, C. and Heathcote, E. (2010), *The Architecture of Hope: Maggie's Cancer Caring Centres,* London: Frances Lincoln Ltd.

13 Jencks, C. (2010), 'The Architecture of Hope', in C. Jencks and E. Heathcote, *The Architecture of Hope: Maggie's Cancer Caring Centres*, 08-43, London: Frances Lincoln Ltd.

14 Ibid.

15 Rose, S. (2010), 'Maggie's Centres: Can Architecture Cure Cancer?' *The Guardian,* 6 May. Available online: http://www.theguardian.com/artanddesign/2010/may/06/maggies-centres-cancer-architecture (accessed 9 July 2015).

16 Holland, C. (2011), 'Questions of Taste' in C. Jencks and FAT (eds), in *AD. Radical Post-Modernism.* September/October, 81(5): 90–7.

17 Baudrillard, J. ([1968] 2005), *The System of Objects,* trans. J. Benedict, London and New York: Verso.

18 Kesselskramer (n.d.), '100 FAQ', *Kesselskramer.* Available at: http://www.kesselskramer.com/contact (accessed 13 September 2016).

Chapter Five: Special effects: interior space and experiences

1 Pallasmaa, *The Eyes of the Skin: Architecture and the Senses,* 31.

2 Baudrillard, J. (1999), 'Truth or Radicality? The Future of Architecture', in S. Redhead (ed.), (2008), *The Jean Baudrillard Reader,* 171–85, Edinburgh: Edinburgh University Press.

3 Merleau-Ponty, M. (1964), 'An Unpublished Text by Maurice Merleau-Ponty: A Prospectus of his Work', in J. M. Edie (ed.), *The Primacy of Perception,* trans. A. B. Dallery, introduction by J. M. Edie, 03–11, United States: Northwestern University Press.

4 Griffero, *Atmospheres: Aesthetics of Emotional Spaces*, 10.

5 Pr Mammoth NYC (2009), [pdf] *'Imaginarium of Doctor Parnassus Production Notes.'* Available online: http://pr.mammothnyc.com/theimaginariumofdrparnassus/presskit.pdf notes p.09 (accessed 7 November 2015).

6 Wanders, M. (2008), 'Mandarina Duck', *Marcel Wanders.* Available online: http://www.marcelwanders.com/interiors/mandarina-duck/ (accessed 13 January 2016).

7 Bainbridge, C. (2007), *The Cinema of Lars Von Trier: Authenticity and Artifice*, London: Wallflower Press.

8 Ibid.

9 Simons, J. (2007), [e-book] *Playing the Waves: Lars Von Trier's Game Cinema,* Amsterdam: Amsterdam University Press. Available online: http://site.ebrary.com/lib/falmouth/detail.action?docID=10281440 (accessed 13 November 2015).

10 Debo, K. (2008), *Maison Martin Margiela '20' the Exhibition,* Antwerp: MoMu.

11 Ibid.

12 Dercon, C. (2008), 'Fashion like the Dark Side of the Moon: The Moon Ray', in I. Luna (ed.), (2009), insert between 136–7, *Maison Martin Margiela.* New York: Rizzoli.

13 Campaign. (2015), 'Selfridges & Co., Fragrance Lab', *Campaign Design.* Available online: http://www.campaigndesign.co.uk/new-page-4/ (accessed 7 November 2015).

14 Kucharek, J. C. (2012*), 'Aesthestic Scents', *RIBA Journal,* 1 January. Available online: http://www.ribaj.com/culture/aesthetic-scents (accessed 15 November 2015). *This article appears to have been posted with the wrong date as the project was realized in 2014.

15 Carringer, R. L. (1985), *The Making of Citizen Kane,* Berkeley, Los Angeles, London: University of California Press.

16 Ibid.

17 Ibid.

18 Bompas, S. and Parr, H. (2010), *Jelly with Bompas & Parr,* London: Pavilion Books.

19 Bompas + Parr. (2015), 'About – Bompas + Parr', *Bompas and Parr.* Available at: http://bompasandparr.com/about (accessed 15 November 2015).

20 Bompas and Parr, *Jelly with Bompas & Parr,* 152.

21 Jacob, S. (2009), 'Alcoholic Architecture', *Icon Eye,* 14 August. Available online: http://www.iconeye.com/opinion/review/item/4065-alcoholic-architecture (accessed 22 November 2015).

22 Pallasmaa, J. (2014), 'Space, Place and Atmosphere: Peripheral Perception in Existential Experience', in C. Borch (ed.), *Atmospheres: On the Experience and Politics of Architecture,* 18–41, Basel: Birkhäuser.

Chapter Six: Light and shadow: uncovering its dramatic role

1 Tanizaki, *In Praise of Shadows,* 20–1.

2 Phillips, G. D. (2010), [e-book] *Some Like it Wilder: The Life and Controversial Films of Billy Wilder,* Kentucky: The University Press of Kentucky. Available online: https://www.dawsonera.com/readonline/9780813173672 (accessed 30 October 2015).

3 Howard, J. (1999), *Stanley Kubrick Companion,* London: B.T. Batsford.

4 Tanizaki, *In Praise of Shadows,* 35.

5 Eisner, L. H. ([1964] 1973), *Murnau,* trans. G. Mander, revised and enlarged, London: Martin Secker & Warburg.

6 Roberts, I. (2008), *German Expressionist Cinema: The World of Light and Shadow,* London: Wallflower Press.

7 Eisner, L. H. ([1952] 1969), *The Haunted Screen: Expressionism in the German Cinema.* Eng. trans. R. Greaves, London: Thames and Hudson.

8 Birnbaum, D. (2002), 'Interview: Daniel Birnbaum in conversation with Olafur Eliasson', in M. Grynsztejn, D. Birnbaum and M. Speaks, *Olafur Eliasson,* 06–33, London: Phaidon Press.

9 May, S. (ed.) (2003), *Olafur Eliasson: The Weather Project*, London: Tate Publishing.

10 Grynsztejn, M. (2007) '(Y)our Entanglements: Olafur Eliasson, The Museum, and Consumer Culture', in M. Grynsztejn (ed.), *Take Your Time: Olafur Eliasson,* 11–31, New York: Thames and Hudson.

11 Eliasson, O. (2003), 'Museums are Radical', in S. May (ed.), *Olafur Eliasson: The Weather Project,* 129–38, London: Tate Publishing.

12 Holl, S. (2006), 'Phenomenal Zones', in Holl, S., Pallasmaa, J. and Pérez-Gómez, A., *Questions of Perception: Phenomenology of Architecture*, 47–120, Tokyo: a+ u Publishing.

13 Ibid.

14 Safront-Tria, J. (2012), 'The Autonomy of Colour', in Safont-Tria, J., Kwinter, S. and Holl, S., *Steven Holl: Colour, Light, Time*, 19–63, Zurich: Lars Müller Publishers.

15 Hemming, S. (2013), 'Sam Wanamaker Playhouse: Theatre by Candlelight', *The Financial Times,* 20 December. Available online: http://www.ft.com/cms/s/2/4367e99a-5ea1-11e3-8621-00144feabdc0.html (accessed 27 November 2015).

16 Tichenor, J. and Walton, J. (2012), [video] 'Choreographing Public Spaces to tell Stories, James Tichenor and Josh Walton, Rockwell Group' *PSFK.* 14 October, posted by K. Summerson. Available online: http://www.psfk.com/2012/10/rockwell-labs-psfk-london-video.html (accessed 16 October 2015).

17 Rockwell, D. (2014), *What If…?: The Architecture and Design of David Rockwell,* C. Pearlman (ed.), New York: Metropolis Books.

18 Core 77 Design Awards (2011), 'The Cosmopolitan of Las Vegas, Question and Answer', *Core 77 Design Awards.* Available online: http://www.core77designawards.com/2011/recipients/the-cosmopolitan-of-las-vegas/ (accessed 9 October 2015).

19 Rockwell, *What If…?: The Architecture and Design of David Rockwell,* 302.

20 Tichenor, J. and Walton, J., 'Choreographing Public Spaces to tell Stories, James Tichenor and Josh Walton, Rockwell Group'.

Chapter Seven: Colour: a Technicolor© inner world

1 Itten, J. (1970), *The Elements of Colour: A Treatise on the Colour System of Johannes Itten based on his book The Art of Colour,* F. Birren (ed.), trans. E. V. Hagen, with a foreword and evaluation by Faber Birren, New York: Van Nostrand Reinhold Company.

2 Birren, F. (1969), 'Psychological Implications of Colour and Illumination', in the *Journal of Illuminating Engineering Society,* 1 May. Available online: https://www.brikbase.org/content/psychological-implications-color-and-illumination (accessed 30 March 2016).

3 Ferrill, M. (2001), *TRAAST + GRUSON Exposed: Frame Monographs of Contemporary Interior Architects,* Basel: Birkhäuser and Amsterdam: Frame Magazine.

4 Warhol, A. and Hackett, P. ([1981] 1996), *Popism: The Warhol '60s,* London: Pimlico.

5 Lewis, A. (2010), *The Great Lady Decorators: The Women who Defined Interior Design, 1870–1955*, New York: Rizzoli.

6 Varney, C. (1988), *The Draper Touch: The High Life and High Style of Dorothy Draper*, New York: Shannongrove Press.

7 Mentjens, M. (2005), 'Restaurant Witloof, Maastricht', *Maurice Mentjens.* Available online: http://mauricementjens.com/en/project/witloof (accessed 25 March 2016).

8 Birren, 'Psychological Implications of Colour and Illumination', 399.

9 Siegel, J. (1990), 'Greenaway by Numbers', in V. Gras and M. Gras (eds), (2000), *Peter Greenaway Interviews,* 66–90, Jackson: University Press of Mississippi.

10 Ibid.

11 Woods, A. (1996), *Being Naked Playing Dead: The Art of Peter Greenaway,* Manchester: Manchester University Press.

12 Panton, V. (1997), *Notes on Colour,* trans. M. Malone and D. H. Silver, Copenhagen: Danish Design Centre.

13 Epple, S. (2000), 'Verner Panton as an Interior Designer', in A. V. Vegesack and M. Remmele (eds), *Verner Panton: The Collected Works,* trans. P. Carrier, M. Dale, B. Hansen, B. Hauβ, R. Jaene, J. Marsh and J. Taylor-Thorson, 156–201, Weil am Rhein: Vitra Design Museum.

14 Ott, M. (2009), 'Progressive Design for a Progressive Journal: Verner Panton's Interiors for the Spiegel Building in Hamburg', trans. N. Imrie, *Studies in the Decorative Arts,* Fall–Winter 2009–10, 17 (1): 96–122.

15 Panton, *Notes on Colour,* 14.

16 Kusama, Y. ([2002] 2011), *Infinity Net: The Autobiography of Yayoi Kusama.* trans. R. McCarthy, London: Tate Publishing.

17 Ibid.

18 Ibid.

19 Baudrillard, J. and Nouvel, J. ([2000] 2002), *The Singular Objects of Architecture,* trans. R. Bononno, Minneapolis and London: University of Minnesota Press.

20 Ibid.

21 Ibid.

22 Chen, A. (2001), 'Image Maker'. *Interior Design [USA],* October, 72 (12): 266–71.

23 Building Better Healthcare (2012), 'Landmark Ward Revamp aids Dementia Patients', *BBH, Building Better Healthcare,* 19 January. Available online: http://www.buildingbetterhealthcare. co.uk/news/article_page/Landmark_ward_ revamp_aids_dementia_patients/74639 (accessed 20 March 2016).

24 Stanley, E. (ed.), (2013), [pdf] 'Developing Supportive Design for People with Dementia'. *Kingsfund.* Available online: http://www. kingsfund.org.uk/sites/files/kf/field/field_ publication_file/ developing-supportive-design-for-people-with-dementia-kingsfund-jan13_0.pdf (accessed 20 March 2016).

25 Ibid.

26 Birren, F. ([1969] 1988), *Light, Colour & Environment,* 2nd revised edition, West Chester: Schiffer Publishing Ltd.

Bibliography

Albrecht, Donald. *The High Style of Dorothy Draper.* (New York: Museum of the City of New York and Pointed Leaf Press, LLC, 2006).

Alesch, Stephen and Standefer, Robin. *Roman and Williams: Things We Made.* (New York: Rizzoli, 2012).

Bachelard, Gaston. *The Poetics of Space.* (1958, reprint, Eng. trans. Maria Jolas, Boston: Beacon Press, 1992).

Bainbridge, Caroline. *The Cinema of Lars Von Trier: Authenticity and Artifice.* (London: Wallflower Press, 2007).

Baraban, Regina S. 'Far-Out Inns', *Metropolis,* 10, no. 4 (November 1990): 48–53, 74–6.

Barnwell, Jane. *Production Design: Architects of the Screen.* (Short Cuts Series, London and New York: Wallflower Press, 2004).

Barsacq, Léon. *Caligari's Cabinet and other Grand Illusions: A History of Film Design.* Elliott Stein (ed.). (1970, Eng. trans. Michael Bullock, Boston: New York Graphic Society, 1976).

Basulto, David. 'The Ace Hotel, New York/Roman and Williams', *Arch Daily,* 7 March 2010. Available online: http://www.archdaily.com/tag/ace-hotel/ (accessed 9 July 2015).

Baudrillard, Jean. *The System of Objects.* (1968, Eng. trans. James Benedict, London and New York: Verso Books, 2005).

Baudrillard, Jean and Nouvel, Jean. *The Singular Objects of Architecture.* (2000, trans. R. Bononno, Minneapolis and London: University of Minnesota Press, 2002).

Benjamin, Walter. *The Arcades Project.* Paperback edn. (1982, Eng. trans. Howard Eiland and Kevin McLaughlin based upon the German volume edited by Rolf Tiedmann, Cambridge, Massachusetts and London: The Belknap Press of Harvard University Press, 2002).

Bingham, Neil. *The New Boutique: Fashion and Design.* (London and New York: Merrell Publishers Limited, 2005).

Birren, Faber. 'Psychological Implications of Colour and Illumination', in the *Journal of Illuminating Engineering Society*, 1 May 1969. Available online: https://www.brikbase.org/content/psychological-implications-color-and-illumination (accessed 30 March 2016).

Birren, Faber. *Light, Colour and Environment.* 2nd revised edn. (1969, West Chester: Schiffer Publishing Ltd, 1988).

Blaisse, Petra. *Inside Outside.* (Trans. Brian Holmes, Andrew May, Mark Speer and Laura Watkinson, Kayoko Ota [ed.], Rotterdam: NAi Publishers, 2007).

Blomberg, Katja, Waldsee, Haus am and GRAFT (eds). *Distinct Ambiguity: Graft.* (Eng. trans. of Preface Volker Ellerbeck, Berlin: Gestalten, 2011).

Böhme, Gernot. 'Atmospheres as the Fundamental Concept of a New Aesthetics' [pdf], *Thesis Eleven,* 1993, 36. Available online: http://desteceres.com/boehme.pdf (accessed 15 July 2015).

Böhme, Gernot. 'The Art of the Stage Set as a Paradigm for an Aesthetics of Atmosphere', *Ambiances: International Journal of Sensory Environment, Architecture and Urban Space,* 2013. Available online: http://ambiances.revues.org/315 (accessed 15 July 2015).

Böhme, Gernot. *'The Aesthetics of Atmosphere',* (ed. Jean-Paul Thibaud, Abingdon: Routledge, 2017).

Bompas, Sam and Parr, Harry. *Jelly with Bompas & Parr.* (London: Pavilion Books, 2010).

Borch, Christain (ed.). *Architectural Atmospheres: On the Experience and Politics of Architecture.* (Basel: Birkhäuser, 2014).

Bordwell, David and Thompson, Kristin. *Film Art: An Introduction.* 6th edn. (1979, New York: McGraw-Hill Higher Education, 2001).

Bradbury, Dominic. *Iconic Interior: From 1900 to the Present.* (London: Thames & Hudson, 2012).

Brooker, Graeme. *Key Interiors since 1900.* (London: Laurence King Publishing, 2013).

Brownlow, Kevin. *David Lean: A Biography.* (New York: Wyatt Book for St. Martins Press, 1996).

Building Better Healthcare. 'Landmark Ward revamp aids Dementia Patients', 19 January 2012, *BBH, Building Better Healthcare*. Available online: http://www.buildingbetterhealthcare.co.uk/news/article_page/Landmark_ward_revamp_aids_dementia_patients/74639 (accessed 20 March 2016).

Burgess, Anthony. *A Clockwork Orange*. (1962, reprint, Middlesex, New York, Victoria, Ontario and Auckland: Penguin Books, 1982).

Cairns, Graham. *The Architecture of the Screen: Essays in Cinematographic Space*. [e-book] (Bristol and Chicago: Intellect, 2013). Available online: http://site.ebrary.com/lib/falmouth/detail.action?docID=10825865 (accessed 11 July 2016).

Capezzuto, Rita. 'Re-set', *Domus,* 21 September 2012. Available online: http://www.domusweb.it/en/architecture/2012/09/21/re-set.html (accessed 22 June 2015).

Carringer, Robert L. *The Making of Citizen Kane*. (Berkeley, Los Angeles and London: University of California Press Ltd, 1985).

Casciani, Stefano. 'Nuovo Hotel Paradiso', *Domus*, 831, (November 2000): 64–70.

Chen, Aric. 'Image Maker', *Interior Design [USA]*. 72, no. 12 (October 2001): 266–71.

Coates, Nigel. *A.D. Primers: Narrative Architecture*. (Chichester: John Wiley & Sons Ltd, 2012).

Colomina, Beatriz. *Privacy and Publicity: Modern Architecture as Mass Media*. 1st Paperback edn. (1994, Massachusetts: The MIT Press, 1996).

Curtis, William J. R. *Le Corbusier: Ideas and Forms*. Paperback edn. (1986, reprint, London: Phaidon Press Limited, 1992).

Debo, Kaat (ed.). *Maison Martin Margiela '20' the Exhibition*. (Antwerp: MoMu, 2008).

Denari, Neil M. *Gyroscopic Horizons*. (London: Thames & Hudson Ltd, 1999).

Dillon, Brian, Rosenthal, Stephanie, Katoka, Mami and Blackmore, Sue. *Walking in My Mind*. (London: Hayward Publishing, 2009).

Eisner, Lotte H. *The Haunted Screen: Expressionism in the German Cinema*. (1952, Eng. trans. Roger Greaves, London: Thames and Hudson, 1969).

Eisner, Lotte H. *Murnau*. (1964, Eng. trans. Gertrude Mander, revised and enlarged, London: Martin Secker & Warburg Limited, 1973).

Elliot, Bridget and Purdy, Anthony. *Peter Greenaway: Architecture and Allegory*. (Chichester: Academy Editions, 1997).

Etherington-Smith, Meredith. *James Turrell: A Life in Light*. (Paris: Somogy Publishers, 2006).

Ettedgui, Peter. *Production Design & Art Direction*. (Crans-Près-Céligny: Roto Vision SA, 1999).

Fear, Bob. (ed.). *A.D. Architecture + Film II*. London: Wiley Academy, 70, No. 1, (21 January 2000).

Feireiss, Lukas and Klanten, Robert (eds). *Staging Space: Scenic Interiors and Spatial Experiences*. (Berlin: Gestalten, 2010).

Ferrill, Meghan. *TRAAST + GRUSON: Exposed*. (Basel: Birkhäuser and Amsterdam: Frame Magazine, 2001).

Foucault, Michel. *Discipline and Punish: The Birth of the Prison*. (1975, trans. Allan Sheridan, Middlesex: Penguin Books, 1991).

Futagawa, Yukio. *Steven Holl: 1975–1998, Volume 1*. (Tokyo: A.D.A. Edita Co, 2012).

Gamard, Elizabeth Burns. *Kurt Schwitters' Merzbau: The Cathedral of Erotic Misery*. (New York: Princeton Architectural Press, 2000).

Gibbs, John. *Mise-En-Scène: Film Style and Interpretation*. (Short Cuts Series, London: Wallflower Press, 2002).

Goethe, Johann Wolfgang Von. *Theory of Colours,* 2nd edn. (1810 [this edition 1840], Eng. trans. with notes by Charles Lock Eastlake, Cambridge, Massachusetts and London: The MIT Press, 1970).

Govan, Michael, and Kim, Christine Y. *James Turrell: A Retrospective*. (Los Angeles: Los Angeles County Museum of Art and Munich: Prestel Verlag, 2013).

Gras, Vernon and Gras, Marguerite (eds). *Peter Greenaway Interviews*. (Jackson: University Press of Mississippi, 2000).

Greenaway, Peter. *The Cook, The Thief, His Wife and Her Lover*. (Paris: Dis Voir, 1989).

Griffero, Tonino. *Atmospheres: Aesthetics of Emotional Spaces*. [e-book] (2010, Eng. trans. Sarah De Sanctis, Farnham & Burlington: Ashgate Publishing Ltd, 2014). Available online: http://site.ebrary.com/lib/falmouth/reader.action?docID=10861723&ppg=4 (accessed 5 February 2016).

Groskop, Viv. 'How to make a Haunted House', *The Guardian,* 5 February 2012. Available online: https://www.theguardian.com/film/2012/feb/05/woman-in-black-special-effects (accessed 25 July 2016).

Grynsztejn, Madeleine, Birnbaum, Daniel and Speaks, Michael. *Olafur Eliasson.* (London: Phaidon Press Limited, 2002).

Grynsztejn, Madeleine (ed.). *Take Your Time: Olafur Eliasson.* (New York: Thames & Hudson and the San Francisco Museum of Modern Art, 2007).

Guidi, Anna Cestelli. 'The Invisible Materiality of Air', *Ingesidée,* 1998. Available online: http://ingesidee. de/dateien/dokumente/de/hans_hemmert_the_ invisible_materiality_of_air_anna_cestelli_guidi_ cgac_centro_galego_de_arte_contemporanea_ santiago_de_compostella_spain_1998.pdf (accessed 12 July 2015).

Halligan, Fionnuala. *Production Design.* (Lewes: The Ilex Press Limited, 2012).

Hemming, Sarah. 'Sam Wanamaker Playhouse: Theatre by Candlelight', 20 December 2013. *The Financial Times.* Available online: http://www.ft.com/ cms/s/2/4367e99a-5ea1-11e3-8621-00144feabdc0. html (accessed 27 November 2015).

Holl, Steven, Pallasmaa, Juhani and Pérez-Gómez, Andrea. *Questions of Perception: Phenomenology of Architecture.* (Tokyo: a+u Publishing Co, 2006).

Hoptman, Laura, Tatehata, Akira and Kultermann, Udo. *Yayoi Kusama.* (London: Phaidon Press Limited, 2000).

Howard, James. *Stanley Kubrick Companion.* (London: B.T. Batsford Ltd, 1999).

Hudson, Jennifer. *Interior Architecture: From Brief to Build.* (London: Laurence King Publishing, 2010).

Ijeh, Ike. 'Such Stuff as Dreams are Made On: Sam Wanamaker Playhouse', *Building,* 14 January 2014. Available online: http://www.building.co.uk/ such-stuff-as-dreams-are-made-on-sam-wanamaker- playhouse/5065559.article (accessed 27 November 2015).

Ilonie, Laura. 'A Matter of Taste', *Frame,* 12, (2000): 24–33.

Itten, Johannes. *The Art of Colour: The Subjective and Objective Rationale of Colour.* (1961, Eng. trans. Ernst van Haagen, New York: John Wiley & Sons, 1973).

Itten, Johannes. *The Elements of Colour: A Treatise on the Colour System of Johannes Itten based on his book The Art of Colour.* (Edited and with a foreword and evaluation by Faber Birren, Eng. trans. Ernst van Hagen, New York: Van Nostrand Reinhold Company, 1970).

Jacob, Sam. 'Alcoholic Architecture', *Icon Eye,* 14 August 2009. Available online: http://www.iconeye. com/opinion/review/item/4065-alcoholic- architecture (accessed 22 November 2015).

Jencks, Charles and Heathcote, Edwin. *The Architecture of Hope: Maggie's Cancer Caring Centres.* (London: Frances Lincoln Ltd, 2010).

Jencks, Charles and FAT. *AD. Radical Post-Modernism.* 81, No. 5 (September/October 2011).

Krasner, David (ed.). *Theatre in Theory: 1900–2000, an Anthology.* (Oxford: Blackwell Publishing Ltd, 2008).

Kucharek, Jan-Carlos. 'Aesthestic Scents', *RIBA Journal,* 1 January 2012. Available online: http:// www.ribaj.com/culture/aesthetic-scents (accessed 15 November 2015).

Kusama, Yayoi. *Infinity Net: The Autobiography of Yayoi Kusama.* (2002, Eng. trans. Ralph McCarthy, London: Tate Publishing, 2011).

Lacey de, Martha. 'Get High on the Atmosphere at the Vapourised Cocktail bar', *Telegraph,* 5 August 2015. Available online: *http://www.telegraph.co.uk/ food-and-drink/pubs-and-bars/get-high-on-the- atmosphere-at-the-vapourised-cocktail-bar/* (accessed 7 December 2016).

Landy, Michael. *Break Down.* Gerrie van Noord (ed.). (London: Artangel, 2001).

Lawrence, Amy. *The Films of Peter Greenaway.* (1997, reissued, Cambridge: Cambridge University Press, 2009).

Leach, Robert. *Makers of Modern Theatre: An Introduction.* (London and New York: Routledge, 2004).

Lee, Kahi. *Rough Luxe Design: The New Love of the Old.* (New York: Faramech Media LLC, 2011).

Lewis, Adam. *The Great Lady Decorators: The Woman who defined Interior Design, 1870–1955.* (New York: Rizzoli International Publications, Inc, 2010).

Libeskind, Daniel. *Extension to the Berlin Museum with Jewish Museum Department.* Kristin Feiress (ed.). (trans. Annette Wiethüchter, Catherine Emerson, Miriam Magall, Yeheshel Sahar, Jürggen Landeck and Kurt W. Forster, Berlin: Ernst & Sohn, 1992).

LoBrutto, Vincent. *The Filmmaker's Guide to Production Design.* (New York: All Worth Press, 2002).

Luna, Ian (ed.). *Maison Martin Margiela.* (New York: Rizzoli, 2009).

Marshall, Jules. 'My Office is my Castle', *Frame*, 2, (1998): 36–41.

Martin, Adrian. *Mise en Scène and Film Style: From Classical Hollywood to New Media Art*. (Basingstoke: Palgrave Macmillan, 2014).

May, Susan (ed.). *Olafur Eliasson: The Weather Project*. (London: Tate Publishing, 2003).

McDougal, Stuart Y. [ed.]. *Stanley Kubrick's A Clockwork Orange*. (Cambridge: Cambridge University Press, 2003).

Merleau-Ponty, Maurice. *The Primacy of Perception and other Essays on Phenomenological Psychology, the Philosophy of Art, History and Politics*. (Introduction by James M. Edie [ed.], Eng. trans. Arleen B. Dallery, James M. Edie, John Wild, William Cobb, Carleton Dallery, Nancy Metzel and John Flodstrom, USA: Northwestern University Press, 1964).

Merrill, Linda. *The Peacock Room: A Cultural Biography*. (Washington DC: Freer Gallery of Art, Smithsonian Institution; and New Haven and London: Yale University Press, 1998).

Metalworks/Surface Architects (2007). *Architects' Journal*, 29 March, 225 (12): 60–71.

Moreno, Shonquis. 'Memory Mappers', *Frame*, 80, (May/June 2011): 102–111.

Mulvey, Laura. *Citizen Kane*. (1992, reprint, Basingstoke: Palgrave Macmillan and the British Film Institute, 2004).

Muthesius, Stefan. *The Poetic Home: Designing the 19th-Century Domestic Interior*. (London: Thames & Hudson, 2009).

Nesbitt, Judith and Watkins, Jonathan. *Days Like These*. (Tate Publishing, 2003).

Nieswand, Nonie, 'What lies beneath', *Grand Designs*, 75, (May 2010): 92–5.

Ott, Marlene. 'Progressive Design for a Progressive Journal: Verner Panton's interiors for the Spiegel Building in Hamburg', trans. Nicola Imrie in *Studies in the Decorative Arts*, 17, No. 1 (Fall–Winter 2009/10): 96–122.

Pallasmaa, Juhani. *The Eyes of the Skin: Architecture and the Senses*. (London: Academy Editions, 1996).

Pallasmaa, Juhani. *The Architecture of Image: Existential Space in Cinema*. 2nd edn. (2001, Eng. trans. Michael Wynne-Ellis, Helsinki: Rakennustieto Publishing, 2007).

Pallasmaa, Juhani. *Encounters: Architectural Essays*. Peter Mackeith (ed.). (Eng. trans. Diana C. Tullberg and Michael Wynne-Ellis, Helsinki: Rakennustieto Publishing, 2005).

Palmer, R. Barton. *Joel and Ethan Coen*. (Urbana and Chicago: University of Illinois Press, 2004).

Panton, Verner. *Notes on Colour*. (Eng. trans. M. Malone and D. H. Silver, Copenhagen: Danish Design Centre, 1997).

Pascoe, David. *Peter Greenaway: Museums and Moving Images*. (London: Reaktion Books Ltd, 1997).

Philips, Gene D. *Some Like it Wilder: The Life and Controversial Films of Billy Wilder*. [e-book] (Kentucky: The University Press of Kentucky, 2010). Available online: https://www.dawsonera.com/abstract/9780813173672 (accessed 30 October 2015).

Pile, John. *A History of Interior Design*. 2nd edn. (2000, London: Laurence King Publishing, 2005).

Pr Mammoth NYC. 'Imaginarium of Doctor Parnassus Production Notes' [pdf], 2009. Available online: http://pr.mammothnyc.com/theimaginariumofdrparnassus/presskit.pdf notes (accessed 7 November 2015).

Rajagopal, Avinash. 'The Creative Process: Spatial Conversations – Petra Blaisse'. *Metropolis*, 1 March 2013. Available online: http://www.metropolismag.com/March-2013/The-Creative-Process-Spatial-conversations-Petra-Blaisse/ (accessed 3 June 2015).

Redhead, Steve (ed.). *The Jean Baudrillard Reader*. (Edinburgh: Edinburgh University Press Ltd, 2008).

Richter, Hans. *DADA: Art and Anti-Art*. (1965, reprinted, London: Thames and Hudson, 1966).

Roberts, Ian. *German Expressionist Cinema: The World of Light and Shadow*. (London: Wallflower Press, 2008).

Robinson, David. *Das Cabinet Des Dr. Caligari*. (1997, reprint, London: BFI Publishing, 1999).

Rockwell, David. *What If…?: The Architecture and Design of David Rockwell*. Chee Pearlman (ed.). (New York: Metropolis Books, 2014).

Rose, Steve. 'Maggie's Centres: Can Architecture cure Cancer?' *The Guardian*, 6 May 2010. Available online: http://www.theguardian.com/artanddesign/2010/may/06/maggies-centres-cancer-architecture (accessed 9 July 2015).

Rugoff, Ralph, Foster, Hal, Kuo, Michelle, Lange, Christy, and Sherwin, Skye. *The New Décor*. (London: Hayward Publishing, 2010).

Safont-Tria, Jordi, Kwinter, Sanford and Holl, Steven. *Steven Holl: Colour Light Time.* (Zurich: Lars Müller Publishers, 2012).

'Sam Wanamaker Playhouse Press Pack' [pdf], *Shakespeare's Globe,* 2014. Available online: http://www.shakespearesglobe.com/uploads/files/2014/02/sam_wanamaker_playhouse_press_pack_january_2014_final.pdf (accessed 27 November 2015).

Schneider, Bernhard. *Daniel Libeskind: Jewish Museum Berlin.* (Eng. trans. John William Gabriel, Munich, London, New York: Prestel Verlag and Daniel Libeskind, 1999).

Sennett, Robert S. *Setting the Scene: The Great Hollywood Art Directors.* (New York: Harry N. Abrams, Inc, 1994).

Shakespeare, William. *As You Like It*. Albert Gilman (ed.). (1599–1600, revised and updated, New York: Signet Classic, 1963).

Simons, Jan. *Playing the Waves: Lars Von Trier's Game Cinema.* [e-book] (Amsterdam: Amsterdam University Press, 2007). Available online: http://site.ebrary.com/lib/falmouth/detail.action?docID=10281440, (accessed 13 November 2015).

Slotkis, Susan J. *Foundations of Interior Design.* 2nd edn (2005, New York: Fairchild Books, 2013).

Sloven, Rachèl. 'Border Incidents', *Frame*, 49, (March/April 2006): 86–91.

Smith, Anna. 'Wes Anderson, the Film-Director who designs Just-So Stories', *The Guardian*, 25 February 2014. Available online: https://www.theguardian.com/film/2014/feb/25/wes-anderson-film-design-grand-budapest-hotel (accessed 25 July 2016).

Snodin, Michael (ed.). *Horace Walpole's Strawberry Hill.* (The Lewis Walpole Library, Yale University, Yale Centre for British Art, Victoria and Albert Museum; and New Haven and London: Yale University Press, 2009).

Spiller, Neil (ed.). *A.D. Integrating Architecture.* London: Academy Group Ltd, 66, No. 9/10, September/October (1996).

Stanley, Eleanor (ed.). 'Developing Supportive Design for People with Dementia' [pdf], *Kingsfund,* 2013. Available online: http://www.kingsfund.org.uk/sites/files/kf/field/field_publication_file/developing-supportive-design-for-people-with-dementia-kingsfund-jan13_0.pdf (accessed 20 March 2016).

Steele, Valerie (ed.). *The Berg Companion to Fashion.* (Oxford and New York: Berg, 2010).

Swanson, Carl. 'Comfort Me with Flanges', *New York Magazine.* 10 October 2010. Available online: http://nymag.com/arts/art/features/68825/ (accessed 9 July 2015).

Tanizaki Jun'ichiro. *In Praise of Shadows.* 8th reprint. (1933, Eng. trans. Thomas J. Harper and Edward G. Seidensticker, Stony Creek, USA: Leete's Island Books Inc, 1977).

Taylor, Rachel. *Yayoi Kusama: White Infinity Nets.* (London: Victoria Miro Gallery, 2013).

Toy, Maggie (ed.). *A.D. Architecture & Film.* London: Academy Editions, No. 112, (1994).

Vaikla-Poldma, Tiiu (ed.). *Meanings of Designed Spaces.* (New York: Fairchild Books, 2013).

Varney, Carleton. *The Draper Touch: The High Life & High Style of Dorothy Draper.* (New York: Shannongrove Press, 1988).

Varney, Carleton. *In the Pink, Dorothy Draper: America's most Fabulous Decorator.* (New York: Pointed Leaf Press LLC, 2006).

Vegesack, Alexander Von and Remmele, Mathias (eds). *Verner Panton: The Collected Works.* (Eng. trans. P. Carrier, M. Dale, B. Hansen, B. Hauβ, R. Jaene, J. Marsh and J. Taylor-Thorson, Weil am Rhein: Vitra Design Museum, 2000).

Vickery, Amanda. 'Horace Walpole and Strawberry Hill', *The Guardian.* 20 February 2010. Available online: https://www.theguardian.com/artanddesign/2010/feb/20/horace-walpole-strawberry-hill (accessed 3 June 2015).

Walpole, Horace. *A Description of the Villa at Strawberry Hill.* Facsimile. (1784, with a foreword by Michael Snodin and an introduction by Stephen Clarke, London: Pallas Athene Ltd, 2015).

Warhol, Andy and Hackett, Pat. *Popism: The Warhol '60s.* (1981, London: Pimlico, 1996).

Webster, Patrick (ed.). *Love and Death in Kubrick: A Critical study of the Films from Lolita through Eyes Wide Shut.* (Jefferson: McFarland & Company, 2011).

Weinthal, Lois (ed.). *Toward a New Interior: An Anthology of Interior Design Theory.* (New York: Princeton Architectural Press, 2011).

White, Roger. 'The Great Stylists 2: Horace Walpole', *House and Gardens,* 45, No. 5, (1990): 110–15.

Whitlock, Cathy. *Designs on Film, A Century of Hollywood Art Direction.* (New York: Harper Collins, 2010).

Willoquet-Maricondi, Paula and Alemany-Galway, Mary. *Peter Greenaway's Postmodern/Poststructuralist Cinema.* Revised edn. (Lanham: Scarecrow Press Inc, 2008).

Wood, Ghislaine (ed.). *Surreal Things: Surrealism and Design.* (London: V&A Publications, 2007).

Woods, Alan. *Being Naked Playing Dead: The Art of Peter Greenaway.* (Manchester: Manchester University Press, 1996).

Zoller Seitz, Matt. *The Wes Anderson Collection.* (New York: Abrams, 2013).

Zoller Seitz, Matt. *The Wes Anderson Collection: The Grand Budapest Hotel.* (New York: Abrams, 2015).

Zumthor, Peter. *Atmospheres: Architectural Environments, Surrounding Objects.* (2006, reprint, Eng. trans. Iain Galbraith, Basel: Birkhauser, 2015).

Zumthor, Peter. *Thinking Architecture.* 3rd expanded edn. (1998, Eng. trans. Maureen Oberli-Turner and Catherine Schelbert, Basel: Birkhauser, 2010).

Index

accessories 64–7, 71, 72–3, 82–3, 84, 103
Ace Hotel, New York 72–3, 84
acoustics 56, 62, 104, 107–8
Adam, Ken 115
aesthetics 10, 16–17, 41, 45, 52
 colour 132, 138–9, 145, 148, 153
 light/shadow 111, 131
 props 71, 84–5
 setting 63
 special effects 87, 92
Albers, Josef 136
Albion Barn, Oxford 112–13
Alcoholic Architecture, London 105–7
Alcott, John 115
Alesch, Stephen 72, 85
alienation 95
Allies and Morrison 126–7
ambience 9, 38, 55, 65, 67, 70, 80, 84, 87, 114–15, 127, 130
analogous colours 134
anamorphic distortion 59
Anderson, Wes 24–5
architectural placebo effect 80
art departments 15
Artangel Foundation 76
artificial light 111–12, 114, 120–3, 130
aspect 112
assemblages 15, 33, 71
atmosphere 14–17, 21–3, 27–8, 31–2, 40–1
 colour 132–3, 138, 141, 145, 150, 152–3
 light/shadow 111–14, 116–17, 122, 124, 126, 130–1
 props 67, 71, 74, 79, 84–5
 setting 43, 47–9, 54–6, 62–3
 special effects 87–8, 92, 105, 107–9
auteurs 23

Bachelard, Gaston 17, 19, 85, 130

backdrops 14, 30, 33, 40–63, 71
 colour 133, 139, 149, 153
 light/shadow 116, 123, 131
 props 80
 special effects 88–9
Bang & Olufsen, Milan 90–1
Barbican, London 92–3
baroque 139–40
Barry, John 74
Barry Lyndon 115
Barsacq, Léon 15, 39
Baudrillard, Jean 84–5, 87
Bauhaus 134, 136, 154
Benjamin, Walter 16, 62, 85
Bentham, Jeremy 32
Birbeck Centre for Film and Visual Media Research, London 42–3
Birren, Faber 133, 141, 152, 154
Blaisse, Petra 56–8, 62
Blenheim Palace, Oxfordshire 89
BlueFROG Music Club, Mumbai 114
Böhme, Gernot 17, 38–9, 108
Bompas and Parr 9, 105–8
Borch, Christopher 109
Bordwell, David 22
Bradford Teaching Hospitals NHS Foundation Trust 150
branding 9, 12, 21, 31, 50, 81, 84, 91–2, 108, 131
Break Down, London 76–8, 85
Brecht, Bertolt 94–5
British Institute of Interior Design (BIID) 10
Bryan, John 24
building regulations 10, 12
Burgess, Anthony 74
Burns, Elizabeth 63

The Cabinet of Dr Caligari 24, 48–9, 62
Cairns, Graham 23
Campaign 68–9, 100–2

candlelight 111, 115, 126–7, 130
Carringer, R.L. 103–4
Centraal Museum, Utrecht 136–7
Centre for Contemporary Non-Objective Art, Brussels 90
chapter focus 10, 21, 41, 65, 88, 111, 133
character 15, 18, 23, 27, 34
 colour 138, 143, 147
 light/shadow 119, 125
 principles 37, 39
 props 67, 72, 84
 setting 40, 44, 46
 special effects 95, 100
chiaroscuro 118
choreography 9, 31, 56, 62, 128–9
chroma 134
cinematography 23, 111, 115, 118, 142
Citizen Kane 103–4, 108
A Clockwork Orange 74–5, 84
Coates, Nigel 34–5
Coen Brothers 43
Colomina, B. 32
colour 14–15, 27, 31, 38, 132–54
 analogous colours 134
 colour contrasts 134, 154
 colour theory 133–4, 144
 colour wheel 133–5, 145, 154
 complementary colours 134–7
 cool colours 134, 145, 152
 intermediate colours 134–5
 light/shadow 114, 120
 primary colours 134–5
 projected 123–5, 130
 props 67–8
 secondary colours 134–5
 setting 42, 54, 56, 59
 tertiary colours 134–5
 use of colour 141, 142–5, 147–8, 150–1
 warm colours 134, 145, 152

Combiwerk Delft 67
commercial sector 9, 11–13, 47
complementary colours 134–7
computer-generated imagery (CGI)
        88–9
context 14, 22, 26, 33–4, 39
        colour 141, 142, 144–5, 147–8, 150
        light/shadow 117, 120, 126–7
        props 9, 71, 72, 74, 76, 79, 82
        setting 48, 53, 56, 59
        special effects 93–4, 96, 100, 103,
            105
*The Cook, The Thief, His Wife and Her
        Lover* 142–3
cool colours 134, 145, 152
Le Corbusier 30, 113
corporations 12, 21
The Cosmopolitan, Las Vegas 128–9,
        131
curation 72–3, 84

Dadaism 33
Dalí, Salvador 33–4
daylight 112
D.E. Shaw and Co, New York 123–5
De Wolf style 16
deconstructivism 96
deep focus 103
Denari, Neil M. 46
design companies/consultancies 11,
        65
Dickens, Charles 24
digital light 111, 116, 128–30
Diller + Scofidio 36, 70–1, 116
Diller, Scofidio + Renfro 36, 71, 116
dimensionality 10, 31, 42, 46–7, 59–61
directors 9, 15, 22–4, 48, 74, 103, 115,
        118, 142–3
display 9, 36, 70–1
Dogma 95 manifesto 94
Dogville 94–5, 108
Dorothy Draper and Company 16, 139
Dots Obsession, Hayward Gallery,
        London 146–7
Double Indemnity 113
dramaturgy 87
Draper, Dorothy 16, 139
Draper Touch 16, 139

Droog Design 91
Duchamp, Marcel 33, 82
Dunhill, Alfred 69
Duquette, Tony 66–7

Edie, James M. 109
Eisner, Lotte H. 119, 131
electric light 114
Eliasson, Olafur 120–2, 130
equipment 64–5, 70–1, 76–8, 84–5
ethics 50
Ettedgui, Peter 23
Eword Traast 91, 137
experiences 86–109
expressionism 24, 48–9, 62, 118–19,
        131

Factory, New York 136
FAT 81–4
Fear, Bob 109
Fellini, Federico 34–5
Ferguson, Perry 103
film cameras 9, 15, 22–7, 29–30, 71, 92,
        103, 113, 115, 118
film noir 113
film theory 15, 23–6
First World War 118
fittings 69
fixtures 64–5, 69, 71, 72–3, 79–84
Foucault, Michel 33
Fragrance Lab, Selfridges, London
        100–2, 108
framing 9, 22, 24, 30–1, 103–4, 152
Freud, Sigmund 17, 118
functionality 111, 144
furniture 64–5, 67–8, 71, 72–5, 84
furniture, fixtures and equipment
        (FF&E) 65
further reading 19, 39, 63, 85, 109, 131,
        154
The Future Laboratory 100–2

Gassner, Dennis 43
Gehry, Frank 79–80
generators 38
German expressionism 24, 48–9, 62,
        118–19, 131
Gibbs, John 20, 22, 39

Gilliam, Terry 89
Givaudan 100, 102
Globe Theatre, London 126–7
gloomth 54–5, 62
Goethe, Johann W. von 133–4, 152,
        154
Gothic style 26, 53–5, 62, 67, 82, 119,
        141
GRAFT 59–62
graphics 13, 15, 42, 59, 133–4, 139–41,
        148–9, 152–3
Greenaway, Peter 142–3, 152
Greenbrier Hotel, White Sulphur
        Springs 139
Greenfield, Jon 126–7
Griffero, Tonino 17, 87
Ground Zero, New York 10
Gulliver's Travels 91–2

habituation 9, 65–6, 68
Hage, Rabih 50–2, 62
Hals, Frans 143
Handford, Philip 102
Hanson, Eric 109
Hayward Gallery, London 146–7
health and safety 11
Hearst, William R. 103
Hemmert, Hans 44
Hempel, Anouska 69
The Hemple, London 69
Hill, Susan 67
Hirst, Damien 43–4
Holl, Steven 123–5, 130–1
Holland, Charles 81
Hollywood 48, 66, 136
Holocaust 37
home-styling shops 11
The Hotel, Lucerne 148–9
hue 134
Hue-Williams, Hugh 112–13

i29 67
identity 41–2, 62, 66, 147, 152
ideology 76
illusion/illusory space 87–90, 93, 96–9,
        108–9, 120, 148
The Imaginarium of Doctor Parnassus
        89

implied space 88, 90–1, 93–5, 108
Inside Outside 56–7
Installation Art 34, 63, 69, 71, 76–7, 90, 93, 112–13, 116, 138, 141, 147
interior architects 10–14, 67
interior decoration 9, 11–14, 28
interior decorators 10–14, 16, 136
interior design 10–13, 18, 27–37, 49, 88–9
interior designers 10–13, 18
interior mise-en-scène 26, 102, 122, 127, 129–31
   atmosphere 9–10, 13–15
   colour 132–3, 145, 147, 151, 153
   definition 22–3, 27
   elements 27, 38
   examples 47, 71, 93, 117, 141, 152
   film theory 24–5
   introduction 21–2
   narrative 28
   physical 23, 27
   power 21–37
   principles 20–38
   props 64–85
   psychology 27
   revealing 28
   setting 41–63
   special effects 88, 99, 108
   specifications 13
intermediate colours 134–5
International Architecture Exhibition, Venice Biennale 56
International Federation of Interior Architects/Designers (IFI) 10
Internet 18
Itten, Johannes 132–4, 136, 152, 154

Jeckyll, Thomas 45
Jencks, Charles 79–80
Jewish Museum, Berlin 10, 36–7
Jones, Allen 74
Jones, Inigo 126

Kesselkramer, Amsterdam 81–4
Keswick, Maggie 79
kitchenism 80, 84
KU64 Kids Club, Berlin 59–61
Kubrick, Stanley 74, 84, 115

Kusama, Yayoi 146–7, 153
Kwinter, Sanford 131

LAB 128–31
l.a.Eyeworks 46, Los Angeles 46
Lagrange, Jacques 68
Laguerre, Louis 89
Lambie, Jim 138
landscapes 17, 130
Landy, Michael 76–8, 85
layered skin 42–4, 56–8, 62
Lean, David 24, 26
Lee, Kahi 63
Libeskind, Daniel 10, 36–7
light 24–5, 27, 31, 38, 110–31
   artificial light 111–12, 114, 120–3, 130
   atmosphere 14–17
   candlelight 111, 115, 126–7, 130
   colour 133–4, 145
   daylight 112
   digital light 111, 116, 128–30
   electric light 114
   natural light 111–13, 123–5, 130–1
   setting 48, 54, 56
   special effects 108
   use of light/shadow 117, 120, 123, 127, 129
Loos, Adolf 32
Lumière Brothers 29

Maggie's Cancer Caring Centres, Dundee 9, 79–80, 84
La Maison Champs Elysées, Paris 96–9, 108
Maison Martin Margiela 96–9, 108
Mallet-Stevens, Robert 26
Mandarina Duck, London 91–2
manipulated skin 42, 44–5, 53–5, 62
Martin, Adrian 22
masking 118
maximalism 66
Méliès, Georges 29
Mentjens, Maurice 140–1
Merleau-Ponty, Maurice 87, 109
Merzbau 33, 63
Mies Van der Rohe, Ludwig 36
minimalism 16, 69, 71, 90–1, 94–5, 108

mise-en-scène see interior mise-en-scène
modernism 17, 68, 113
mood boards 11
Munsell, Albert H. 134
Munsell Colour System 134
Murnau, F.W. 118–19, 130
Museum of Modern Art (MoMA), New York 70–1

Name, Billy 136
narcissism 136
narrative 23, 25–8, 30, 33–4, 36–8
   atmosphere 9, 14, 18
   colour 141, 143, 145, 147, 149, 151
   light/shadow 116–17, 119, 122, 124, 127, 129
   props 65, 71, 72–3, 75, 77, 80, 83–4
   setting 49–52, 54, 56–7, 60, 62
   special effects 92–3, 95, 99, 102, 104, 107
natural light 111–13, 123–5, 130–1
Neil M. Denari Architects (NMDA) 46
New York Fashion Week 69
Newton, Isaac 134, 154
Nosferatu 118–19, 130
Notre Dame du Haut, Ronchamp 113
Nouvel, Jean 148–9, 153
NY-11-18-02-10, New York 68

palimpsests 52
Pallasmaa, Juhani 17, 19, 23, 108–9
Panopticon 32–3
Panton, Verner 31, 136, 144–5, 152
Para-site, MoMA, New York 70–1
patents 29
pattern 15, 42, 133–4, 138–41, 145–7, 152–3
The Peacock Room, London 45
Pellechet, Julles 96
perceptions 14–15, 17–18, 27, 43, 47–8
   colour 133, 136, 146, 153
   light/shadow 111, 124
   props 67
   special effects 86–8, 90–3, 108
performance 56–7, 63, 76–7, 85, 88, 102, 108, 127, 130
personality 15–16, 44, 65–7, 71

personas 54
phenomenology 18, 87, 123
physicality 9, 22–3, 27–8, 32, 38
    atmosphere 13, 15, 17
    colour 152
    light/shadow 124, 131
    props 65, 71, 73
    setting 41–2, 48, 51, 53, 56, 59, 62
    special effects 88
physiognomy 16
physiology 134, 145, 152, 154
Playtime 68
pop art 75, 136
post-modernism 82
power of interiors 21–37
primary colours 134–5
ProArtsDesign 91, 137
production designers 9, 15, 23–4, 43,
        48, 67, 74, 84, 115, 142
project management 12
props 22, 24–5, 27, 29–31, 64–85
    atmosphere 14, 16
    colour 147, 151
    light/shadow 120
    principles 34, 38
    setting 49
    special effects 94–5, 103, 108
    use of props 72–4, 76, 80, 82
psychology 21, 23, 26–8, 31–2, 37–8
    atmosphere 17–18
    colour 132–3, 141, 142–3, 145,
        152–4
    light/shadow 111, 113, 117–18,
        124, 129–30
    props 66, 68, 75, 79, 82, 84–5
    setting 43–4, 49, 60, 62–3
    special effects 87–8, 91, 93, 104
Psychosomatic Art 147

Quinn, Kave 67

Rain Room, Barbican, London 92–3
Random International 92–3
Re-Set 56–8
refurbishment 52, 84, 96–7, 139, 141,
        148, 150, 153
Reimann, Walter 48
residential sector 11–12

reuse 12, 50, 68
Rialto Theatre, New York 116
Rietveld, Gerrit 56
Rockwell, David 128
Rockwell Group 128–31
Roelfs, Jan 142
Röhrig, Walter 48, 118
Roman and Williams 72–3, 84–5
Rough Luxe Hotel, London 50–2, 62
Rough Luxe movement 50–2, 62–3
Royal Infirmary, Bradford 150–2

Safont-Tria, Jordi 131
Sam Wanamaker Playhouse, London
        126–7, 130
scale 88, 91–3, 103–4, 108
scenography 24, 29, 89, 139, 148, 153
Schaal, H.D. 23
Schrager, Ian 31
Schwitters, Kurt 33, 63
Scott, Richard 43
secondary colours 134–5
Seilern Architects 113
Seitz, John F. 113
Selfridges, London 100–2, 108
semiotics 84
sensory space 16, 18, 88, 92–3, 100–2,
        105–8
Serie Architects 114
Serres, Michel 17, 63
setting 22, 24–8, 31–3, 38, 40–63
    atmosphere 9, 14–16
    colour 136
    props 65, 84
    special effects 94–5, 108
shadow 14–16, 24–5, 27, 38, 48, 54,
        108, 110–31
Shakespeare, William 28, 126–7
silhouettes 90–1
site analysis 12
skin of space 14, 26–7, 40–63, 136,
        139
    layered skin 42–4, 56–8, 62
    manipulated skin 42, 44–5, 53–5,
        62
    space planning 10
    styled space 16
    surface skin 42, 48–52, 62

three-dimensional skin 10, 31, 42,
        46–7, 59–62
Skyscape, Albion Barn, Oxford
        112–13
Soft Sell, New York 116
Spacebrew 129
special effects 14, 27, 29–30, 38,
        86–109
spectacle 30–1, 33, 37, 57, 76–7, 85,
        87, 89, 108, 116, 120–2, 129–31
Spiegel Publishing Headquarters,
        Hamburg 144–5
stage sets 20, 22–8, 32, 88, 120
staged space 9, 11, 13–15, 18, 23,
        27–31, 33, 37, 84–5, 95, 100,
        108–9
Standefer, Robin 72, 85
Starck, Philippe 31
Stocker, Esther 90
Stockhausen, Adam 24
Stoker, Bram 118
storytelling 21–3, 25–6, 28, 33, 43
    atmosphere 9, 14–15, 18
    colour 142
    props 84
    setting 52, 59–60, 62–3
    special effects 91
Strawberry Hill, London 53–5, 62
Sturm Gallery 48
stylists 14
Superstars 136
Surface Architects 42
surface skin 42, 48–52, 62
surrealism 33–4, 82, 84, 91–2
surveillance 32–3, 36, 70–1
symbolism 17, 28, 34, 37, 104, 113,
        136, 142, 152

Tanizaki, Jun'ichirō 16–17, 110, 117,
        130–1
Tate Modern, London 43–4, 120–1
Tati, Jacques 68
Tativille 68
temporality 112, 131
tertiary colours 134–5
textiles 11, 41, 43, 56–7, 62, 92, 97,
        144–5
Thackeray, William M. 115

The Theme Rooms, Centraal Museum, Utrecht 136–7
Thompson, Kristin 22
three-dimensional skin 10, 31, 42, 46–7, 59–62
Toland, Greg 103
townscapes 94, 108
TRAAST + GRUSON 9, 91, 136–7
trompe l'œil 53, 55, 88–9, 96–9, 108
Turrell, James 112

upcycling 50
use of colour 140, 142–5, 147–8, 150–1
use of light/shadow 117, 120, 123, 127, 129
use of props 72–4, 76, 80, 82
use of scale 88, 91–3, 103–4, 108
use of special effects 94, 97, 101, 103, 105
user-centred design 13

Van Os, Ben 142
Vanbrugh, John 89
Vierny, Sachs 142
vignettes 140–1
VMX Architects 67
Von Trier, Lars 94–5
voyeurism 33, 36, 70–1, 143, 149

Wagner, Fritz A. 118
Walden, Herwald 48
Walker, Beverley 75
Walking in my Mind, Hayward Gallery, London 146
wallpaper 41–3, 50–3, 55, 92, 97, 139, 141
Walpole, Horace 53–5, 62
Walton, J. 129
Wanders, Marcel 91–2
Wards 23/29, Royal Infirmary, Bradford 150–1

Warhol, Andy 136
warm colours 134, 145, 152
Warm, Hermann 48
The Weather Project 120–2
Webb, John 126
Weinthal, Lois 63
Welles, Orson 103–4
The West Lobby, The Cosmopolitan, Las Vegas 128–9, 131
Whistler, James M. 45
Wiene, Robert 24, 48–9
Wilder, Billy 113
Witloof Restaurant, Maastricht 140–1
Wolfe, Elsie de 66
A Woman in Black 67
Worcester College Library, Oxford 126

Zobop, Museum of Contemporary Art, Sydney 138
Zumthor, Peter 8, 17, 19

Picture credits

Chapter One

1.1   Getty Images/Frank Tanner/Contributor

Chapter Two

2.1   Getty Images/John Kobal Foundation
2.2   Getty Images/Archive Photos/Stringer
2.3   Moviestore/REX/Shutterstock
2.4   Getty Images/John Springer Collection
2.5   Getty Images/Apic
2.6   © FLC/ ADAGP, Paris and DACS, London 2016
2.7   Getty Images/AtlantidePhototravel
2.8   This work is in the public domain
2.9   Getty Images/Quim Llenas
2.10   Edward Valentine Hames
2.11   Edward Valentine Hames
2.12   Diller + Scofidio, interior of Brasserie restaurant, 2000. Photograph by Michael Moran
2.13   Diller + Scofidio, interior of Brasserie restaurant, 2000. Photograph by Michael Moran
2.14   Getty Images/View Pictures
2.15   Getty Images/Jon Hicks

Chapter Three

3.1   Getty Images/Planet News Archive
3.2   Getty Images/View Pictures
3.3   Getty Images/Oli Scarff
3.4   Getty Images/De Agostini Picture Library
3.5   Getty images/George Wilhelm
3.6   Getty Images/Film Collector
3.7   Getty Images/Marcus Peel
3.8   Getty Images/Marcus Peel
3.9   Getty Images/Marcus Peel
3.10   Getty Images/Franz Marc Frei
3.11   Getty Images/Kilian O'Sullivan
3.12   Rob't Hart &FransParthesius
3.13   Rob't Hart &FransParthesius
3.14   Rob't Hart &FransParthesius
3.15   Tobias Hein/ GRAFT Architects
3.16   Tobias Hein/ GRAFT Architects
3.17   Tobias Hein/ GRAFT Architects

Chapter Four

4.1   Getty Images/Haywood Magee
4.2   Getty Images/Shirley C. Burden
4.3   Courtesy of i29 interior architects
4.4   Courtesy of i29 interior architects
4.5   CAMPAIGN
4.6   Kim Zwarts
4.7   Diller + Scofidio, Para-Site installation in Projects Gallery of The Museum of Modern Art, New York, 1989. Photograph by Diller + Scofidio, courtesy of Diller Scofidio + Renfro
4.8   Wendy Connett/REX/Shutterstock
4.9   Wendy Connett/REX/Shutterstock
4.10   Getty Images/Sunset Boulevard
4.11   RAY TANG/REX/Shutterstock
4.12   RAY TANG/REX/Shutterstock
4.13   Getty Images/View Pictures
4.14   Getty Images/View Pictures
4.15   Courtesy of KesselsKramer
4.16   Courtesy of KesselsKramer
4.17   Courtesy of KesselsKramer

Chapter Five

5.1   Getty Images/Fox Photos
5.2   Getty Images/Michael Freeman
5.3   Courtesy of Esther Stocker Studio
5.4   Courtesy of Ewoud Traast and Edith Gruson; Photograph: Ernst Moritz
5.5   An iconic interior by Marcel Wanders for Mandarina Duck, 2008, www.marcelwanders.com
5.6   Getty Images/Oli Scarff
5.7   ZentropaEnts./REX/Shutterstock
5.8   © Martine Houghton
5.9   © Martine Houghton
5.10   © Martine Houghton
5.11   © Martine Houghton
5.12   CAMPAIGN
5.13   CAMPAIGN
5.14   CAMPAIGN
5.15   Getty Images/John Springer Collection
5.16   Bompas & Parr and Marcus Peel

5.17 Bompas & Parr and Ann CharlottOmmedal
5.18 Bompas & Parr and Ann CharlottOmmedal

Chapter Six
6.1   Getty Images/John Kobal Foundation
6.2   Getty Images/Ed Reeve
6.3   Photo by Fram Petit
6.4   Getty Images/Michael Ochs Archives
6.5   Diller + Scofidio, Soft Sell (Times Square), New York City, 1993. Photograph by Michael Moran, courtesy of Diller Scofidio + Renfro
6.6   Getty Images/UllsteinBild
6.7   Getty Images/Peter Macdiarmid
6.8   Getty Images/Mike Kemp
6.9   Getty Images/View Pictures
6.10 Getty Images/View Pictures
6.11 Geraint Lewis/REX/Shutterstock
6.12 Getty Images/Robbie Jack – Corbis
6.13 Getty Images/Wally Skalij

Chapter Seven
7.1   Getty Images/Planet News Archive
7.2   Getty Images/NNehring
7.3   Courtesy of Ewoud Traast and Edith Gruson; Photgraph: Ernst Moritz
7.4   Getty Images/El Pics
7.5   Courtesy of Dorothy Draper & Company Inc. Photographer: Michel Arnaud
7.6   Courtesy of Dorothy Draper & Company Inc. Photographer: Michel Arnaud
7.7   Courtesy of Maurice Mentjens. Photographer: Arjen Schmitz
7.8   Courtesy of Maurice Mentjens. Photographer: Arjen Schmitz
7.9   Getty Images/Mondadori Portfolio
7.10 Getty Images/UllsteinBild
7.11 Verner Panton Design
7.12 Getty Images/John Phillips
7.13 Architectures Jean Nouvel. Photo: Philippe Ruault
7.14 Architectures Jean Nouvel. Photo: Philippe Ruault
7.15 Jason Joy, Bradford Teaching Hospitals
7.16 Jason Joy, Bradford Teaching Hospitals

Acknowledgements

I would like to proffer a special thank you to all the staff at Bloomsbury who kept this book on track and on schedule, especially James Piper for his astute editorial advice and Georgia Kennedy for her wise words in times of crisis. Special mention must be made of Renée Last as the Picture Researcher whose ability to track down obscure images is second to none. Many thanks to all the designers, artists, architects and individuals who kindly contributed to the images contained in this book – it would be a much poorer read without your generosity. Finally, I would like to thank all the library staff at Falmouth University for their help over my endless requests for inter-library loans.